THE HONEY COOKBOOK

BY

CHARLOTTE POPESCU

CAVALIER COOKBOOKS

An imprint of Cavalier Paperbacks

© Charlotte Popescu 1997

Published by Cavalier Cookbooks 1997
Reprinted 2001, 2003, 2006, 2010

An imprint of Cavalier Paperbacks
Burnham House,
Upavon,
Wilts SN9 6DU

www.cavalierpaperbacks.co.uk

Cover illustration by Beverley Lees

ISBN 978-1-899470-35-8

Printed and bound in Great Britain by Cox & Wyman,
Cardiff Road, Reading, Berks

CONTENTS

INTRODUCTION

Honey is a natural ingredient that has had several uses since ancient times. Ancient civilizations called honey the food of the gods and honey was used in food as a preservative and as an antiseptic. The ancient Egyptians were keen bee-keepers who built bee-hives and used honey in many of their rituals including the ceremonial burials of their dead. When the tomb of Queen Tyi's parents was opened, a jar of honey was found in perfect condition. It was 3,300 years old! The Greeks and Romans used honey in bread, cakes and sweets. Germs cannot survive for long in honey and properly stored, honey will last indefinitely. The Ancients realised this and so used honey to preserve many foods including nuts and fruits. They also discovered that honey helped heal wounds and burns, and soothed pain. Honey was believed to be a natural sedative. More recently it has also been found to be beneficial in curing stomach ailments, asthma and anaemia and in soothing coughs.

In Britain bee-keeping is an ancient tradition and long ago mead was the national drink. For hundreds of years honey was the only sweetener available until sugar came from the West Indies in the 1500s.

Today there are many types of honey available with different textures, aromas and colours. Many of the supermarkets sell clear or set "blended honey", often a mixture of honeys from different countries. Their taste is often bland and the set honeys have sometimes been chemically treated to thicken them whilst the clear honeys have been treated to prevent them becoming hard. Pure honey straight from the bee-hives starts its life runny and sets gradually. Not everyone realises that if you gently heat pure honey it will become clear again. Most people have heard of some of the better known varieties of honey such as Acacia, Heather, Lavender, Orange Blossom (often from Mexico), Clover, Manuka (a dark, expensive honey from New Zealand) and Eucalyptus (from Australia). There are also many less well known varieties such as Horse Chestnut, Rosemary and Hymmetus (from Greece). You can buy pleasant-tasting honey from local farm shops or direct from bee-keepers.

Finally, The Hive, at 53 Webbs Road, London SW11 6RX sells everything imaginable to do with bees and infinite varieties of honey - it is well worth a visit.

Notes for the cook

If you have a fan assisted electric oven reduce the specified heat in the recipes by 10 - 20°C.

1 teaspoon = 5ml

1 tablespoon = 15ml

Honey in the recipes has been measured in tablespoons or grams (pounds) and cups. Some equivalents in ml (fl oz) are given here.

75g, 3oz (¼ cup) = 60ml, 2fl oz

100g, 4oz (¹/₃ cup) = 90ml, 3fl oz

150g, 6oz (½ cup) = 120ml, 4fl oz

225g, 8oz (¾ cup) = 180ml, 6fl oz

STARTERS AND APPETISERS

Honey Glazed Bacon Rolls

Perky Peppers

Avocado with Honey and Capers

Cheesy Pineapple with Ginger and Honey

Ham Salad with Honey Mustard Dressing

Carrot and Parsnip Soup

Green Cabbage Parcels

HONEY GLAZED BACON ROLLS

These make an unusual appetiser to hand round at a drinks party.

Makes 8 rolls

5 spring onions, cut into sticks
some baby corn
some carrots
some mange tout
225g, 8oz rindless streaky bacon
3 tbsp honey
2 tbsp soya sauce

Cut the vegetables up. Stretch out each piece of bacon and roll a few mixed vegetables up in each one. Secure with a cocktail stick. Place in a roasting tin. Mix together the soya sauce and honey and spoon over the bacon rolls. Cook in the oven at gas mark 6, 200˚C (400˚F) for 30 minutes.

PERKY PEPPERS

This dish of peppers makes a succulent first course for a dinner party or for a vegetarian feast.

Serves 6 - 8

2 red peppers, halved and deseeded
2 yellow peppers, halved and deseeded
some spring onions, cut into small slices
4 tbsp soya sauce
4 tbsp lemon juice
2 tbsp clear honey
1 tbsp white wine vinegar

Place the peppers, cut side down, under a hot grill for about 15 minutes, by which time the skins should be black. Cool and peel the skins off the peppers. Mix together the spring onions, soya sauce, lemon juice, honey and vinegar and pour over the peppers.

AVOCADO WITH HONEY AND CAPERS

The honey and capers make a tasty addition to the more usual vinaigrette served with avocado pears.

Serves 8

4 avocado pears
3 tbsp olive oil
1 tbsp lemon juice
1 tbsp clear honey
1 tbsp capers, chopped
1 clove of garlic, peeled and crushed
salt and pepper

Mix together the oil, lemon juice, honey, capers, garlic, salt and pepper in a jam jar and shake well with the lid on. Halve the avocados and take the stones out. Arrange half an avocado on each plate and pour some dressing onto each one.

CHEESY PINEAPPLE WITH
GINGER AND HONEY

This pineapple starter, with the sweet and savoury flavours of honey and cheese, makes an interesting combination.

Serves 4

4 fresh pineapple slices
2.5cm (1in) fresh root ginger
1 tbsp clear honey
150g, 6oz (²/₃ cup) curd cheese
1 tbsp soured cream
1 tbsp chopped chives
1 tbsp lemon juice
3 tbsp olive oil

Peel and grate the ginger and place in a dish with the honey and pineapple. Chill for about an hour. Combine the cheese and soured cream and stir in the chives. Take the pineapple out of the honey and place on serving plates. Stir lemon juice and oil into the honey mixture and spoon over the pineapple and cheese.

HAM SALAD WITH
HONEY MUSTARD DRESSING

Serves 2 - 4

450g, 1lb ham, cubed
225g, 8oz eating apples, peeled, cored and diced
2 hard boiled eggs, sliced
225g, 8oz cooked new potatoes, chopped
1 bulb florence fennel, chopped
fresh chopped parsley
mixed salad leaves

Dressing

3 tbsp white wine vinegar
2 tbsp wholegrain mustard
2 tbsp clear honey
180ml, 6 fl oz (¾ cup) olive oil
salt and pepper

To make the dressing, shake all the ingredients together in a jam jar with the lid on. Put the ham, apple, eggs, new potatoes, fennel and parsley in a dish over a bed of salad leaves. Pour the dressing over the ham salad and serve.

CARROT AND PARSNIP SOUP

Serves 4 - 6

2 cooking apples, peeled, cored and chopped
225g, 8oz onions, peeled and chopped
a knob of butter
1 bay leaf
1 litre, 2pts (5 cups) chicken stock
450g, 1lb carrots, peeled and chopped
450g, 1lb parsnips, peeled and chopped
1 tbsp honey
salt and pepper
a squeeze of lemon juice
parsley

Fry the apples and onions in a little butter. Make up the stock, add the bay leaf and cook the carrots in it for 3 or 4 minutes before adding the parsnips, apples and onions. Cook for a further 5 minutes. Remove the bay leaf and liquidise the soup. Return to the heat and add the honey, seasoning and a squeeze of lemon juice. Garnish with parsley.

GREEN CABBAGE PARCELS

Serves 4

100g, 4oz (²/₃ cup) cooked brown rice
100g, 4oz (²/₃ cup) raisins
50g, 2oz (½ cup) almonds, chopped
1 cooking apple, peeled, cored and chopped
2 tbsp clear honey
3 tbsp orange juice
1 tsp grated orange rind
cabbage leaves

Sauce

150ml, ¼pt (²/₃ cup) chicken stock
3 tbsp orange juice

Mix together the rice, raisins, almonds, apple, honey and orange juice and rind. Spread the cabbage leaves out flat and place a spoonful of the filling in the centre of each leaf. Wrap each one up into a parcel. Place each cabbage parcel in a shallow ovenproof dish. Mix together the orange juice and stock and pour over the parcels. Cover the dish with foil and bake in the oven at gas mark 4, 180°C (350°F) for 45 minutes.

MAIN COURSES

Honey Glazed Roast Lamb
Honeyed Lamb
Lamb with Redcurrant and Honey Sauce
Lamb Chops with Wine and Honey
Sticky Chicken
Chicken with Honey, Mint and Ginger
Honey Grilled Chicken with Grapes and Almonds
Mustard Glazed Chicken
Honey and Ginger Drumsticks
Chicken Breasts with Citrus Sauce
Honey and Lemon Roast Chicken
Chicken in Honey and Curry Mayonnaise
Honeyed Chicken and Herb Salad
Barbecued Turkey Kebabs
Spicy Turkey and Noodles
Duck with Honey and Grape Sauce
Persian Duck Breasts
Venison Steaks with Honey and Yoghurt Sauce
Gammon with Honey Glaze
Sweet and Sour Bacon Slices
Pork Chops with Honey and Cider
Barbecued Spare Ribs
Sweet and Sour Meatballs
Cod in Sweet and Sour Sauce
Honey Grilled Trout
Salmon with Lime and Honey

HONEY GLAZED ROAST LAMB

This is a delicious way to roast lamb, especially in the summer with fresh herbs from the garden. Serve with new potatoes and a selection of vegetables.

Serves 8

1.8kg, 4lb leg of lamb, boned
4 tbsp set honey
2 cloves of garlic, peeled and sliced
6 tbsp chopped parsley
6 tbsp chopped thyme
3 tbsp chopped rosemary
salt and pepper

Mix together half the honey with the garlic and half of the herbs. Place in the lamb cavity and secure with skewers. Spread the remaining honey over the lamb, sprinkle with the remaining herbs and season with salt and pepper. Cook in the oven at gas mark 3, 160°C (325°F) for two hours, basting occasionally.

HONEYED LAMB

An appetising winter casserole. Serve with baked potatoes and broccoli.

Serves 4

675g, 1½lb lamb, cubed
2 onions, peeled and sliced
2 carrots, peeled and sliced
½ tsp thyme
120ml, 4fl oz (½ cup) sweet cider
2 tbsp clear honey
1 tbsp red wine vinegar
salt and pepper
14g, ½oz (1 tbsp) butter
2 tsp flour

Put the cubed lamb, onion, and carrots into a casserole. Sprinkle on the thyme. Heat the cider and honey, then stir in the vinegar and pour this sauce over the meat. Add salt and pepper. Cover and cook in the oven at gas mark 4, 180°C (350°F) for 1 hour. Beat together the butter and flour and stir into the casserole. Return to the oven for another 15 minutes.

LAMB WITH REDCURRANT
AND HONEY SAUCE

The redcurrant and honey sauce is unusual but delicious
served with these lamb steaks.

Serves 4

4 lamb steaks
2 tbsp sunflower oil
1 onion, peeled and chopped
1 tsp ground ginger
2 tbsp red wine
300ml, ½pt (1¼ cups) chicken stock
50g, 2oz redcurrants
100g, 4oz mushrooms
1 tbsp honey
1 tbsp fresh chopped mint

Brown the lamb steaks in the oil in a frying pan, add the onions
and ginger and cook for 10 minutes. Slice the mushrooms and
stir into the onions. Cook for 2 or 3 minutes. Pour the wine,
and stock onto the mushrooms and stir in the redcurrants and
honey. Simmer for 5 minutes. Serve straight away, garnished
with fresh chopped mint.

LAMB CHOPS WITH
WINE AND HONEY

Serves 6

6 lamb chops
2 tbsp sunflower oil
1 clove of garlic, peeled and crushed
150g, 6oz mushrooms, sliced
2 courgettes, sliced
4 tomatoes, chopped
2 tbsp honey
150ml, ¼pt (²/₃ cup) red wine
1 tbsp marjoram
1 tbsp parsley
salt and pepper
croutons

Fry the chops first in the oil in a casserole. Add the garlic, mushrooms and courgettes and fry for a couple of minutes. Then add the tomatoes, honey, wine, marjoram, salt and pepper. Cover the casserole and cook in the oven at gas mark 4, 180°C (350°F) for 40 minutes. Garnish with the chopped parsley and croutons if liked. To make the croutons, chop up a couple of slices of bread and fry in butter or oil in a frying pan until crisp. While still sizzling sprinkle over the lamb before serving.

STICKY CHICKEN

This is a firm favourite with the children.

Serves 6

75g, 3oz (¹/₃ cup) butter
3 tbsp honey
3 garlic cloves
6 chicken breasts with skin and bone
salt and pepper
parsley

Place the butter and honey in a saucepan and cook over a low heat, stirring for about 1 minute until the butter has melted. Slice the garlic and push under the skin of each chicken breast. Put in a roasting tin and brush with the honey mixture. Season with salt and pepper. Cook in the oven at gas mark 5, 190°C (375°F) for 40 minutes. Garnish with the parsley.

CHICKEN WITH HONEY, MINT AND GINGER

This is an easy chicken dish to prepare and is suitable for the whole family.

Serves 4

4 chicken pieces
3 tbsp olive oil
2 tbsp fresh chopped mint
2 tbsp chopped rosemary
2 cloves of garlic, peeled and chopped
freshly ground black pepper
2.5cm (1in) root ginger
150g, 6oz mushrooms, sliced
2 tsp soya sauce
1 tbsp honey
1 tbsp olive oil
1 tbsp chopped parsley

Fry the chicken pieces in 2 tablespoons of the oil until brown and place in an ovenproof dish. Sprinkle the mint, rosemary, garlic, ginger and pepper on both sides of the chicken. Arrange the mushrooms around the chicken. Spoon over the soya sauce, honey and remaining oil. Cover the dish with foil and cook at gas mark 4, 180°C (350°F) for 1 hour. Remove the foil and cook for a further 30 minutes before serving, garnished with the chopped parsley.

HONEY GRILLED CHICKEN
WITH GRAPES AND ALMONDS

Serves 4

4 chicken pieces
1 tbsp honey
1 tbsp sherry
1 tbsp soya sauce
25g, 1oz (¼ cup) flaked almonds
12 seedless green grapes
knob of butter

Grill or barbecue the chicken pieces for 20 minutes. Mix the honey, sherry and soya sauce and brush over the chicken. Barbecue for another 20 minutes. Toss the almonds and grapes in a pan with the butter and serve over the chicken.

MUSTARD GLAZED CHICKEN

This makes a tasty and quickly prepared dish.

Serves 4

75g, 3oz (¹/₃ cup) butter
1 tbsp honey
2 tbsp mixed grain mustard
4 chicken pieces
salt and pepper

Put the butter, honey, mustard and seasoning in a bowl and mix together. Pierce the pieces of chicken with a skewer and put them skin side down on a grill pan. Spread with the butter mixture and grill for 20 minutes on each side, basting frequently. Pour the juices over the chicken and serve.

HONEY AND GINGER DRUMSTICKS

Serves 2

50g, 2oz (¼ cup) butter
2 tbsp honey
1 tbsp vinegar
¼ tsp thyme
4 chicken drumsticks
2 tsp ground ginger
salt and pepper

Melt the butter in a small saucepan. Add the honey, vinegar and thyme. Rub the drumsticks with the ginger, salt and pepper and place on a plate. Pour over the honey mixture and leave to absorb the flavours for 20 minutes. Cook for 30 minutes on a barbecue or under a grill, turning the drumsticks and basting them every so often with the honey marinade.

CHICKEN BREASTS
WITH CITRUS SAUCE

Serves 4

4 chicken breasts
1 tbsp clear honey
2 tbsp sunflower oil
juice and rind of 1 small orange
150ml, ¼pt (²/₃ cup) chicken stock
1 tbsp lemon juice
1 tbsp white wine vinegar
a pinch of ground cloves
1 tbsp soya sauce
½ tsp cornflour
knob of butter

Brush the chicken breasts with some of the honey. Fry in the oil in a pan until brown on all sides. Pour the stock and orange juice into the pan and add the rest of the honey, orange rind, lemon juice, vinegar, pinch of cloves and soya sauce. Bring to the boil and pour over the chicken. Cover and bake in the oven at gas mark 4, 180°C (350°F) for 40 minutes. Remove the chicken from the dish and pour the sauce into a saucepan. Boil rapidly to reduce. Mix some cornflour with a little water to make a paste. Add this to the sauce to thicken it and add a knob of butter. Pour the sauce back over the chicken breasts and serve at once.

HONEY AND LEMON
ROAST CHICKEN

These chicken pieces are very succulent and enjoyed by children and adults alike. You can always use chicken breasts for this recipe if preferred.

Serves 6

2 onions, peeled
6 chicken pieces
1 lemon thinly sliced
grated rind and juice of 1 lemon
2 tbsp balsamic vinegar
2 tbsp sherry vinegar
4 tbsp clear honey
5 tbsp olive oil

Slice the onions and place with the lemon slices in the bottom of a roasting tin along with the chicken. Whisk together the lemon juice and rind, vinegars, honey and oil in a bowl and pour over the chicken. Cook in the oven at gas mark 6, 200°C (400°F) for 40 minutes, basting every so often. Remove the chicken and keep warm. Boil the juices in the roasting tin until the liquid is reduced and syrupy. Spoon over the chicken and serve.

CHICKEN IN HONEY AND
CURRY MAYONNAISE

This dish is a popular choice for a cold buffet.

Serves 6 - 8

1.5kg, 3lb cooked chicken, cut into pieces
1 onion, peeled and chopped
1 tbsp sunflower oil
1 tbsp tomato purée
1 tbsp curry powder
120ml, 4fl oz (½ cup) chicken stock
juice of ½ lemon
1 tbsp honey
300ml, ½pt (1¼ cups) good mayonnaise
150ml, ¼pt (²/₃ cup) double cream
chopped parsley

Cook the onion in the oil for a few mintues. Stir in the curry powder, stock, tomato purée, lemon juice, and honey. Simmer for a few more minutes. Leave to cool and stir in the mayonnaise and cream. Arrange the chicken on a serving plate, cover with the sauce and garnish with parsley.

HONEYED CHICKEN
AND HERB SALAD

This is another way of serving chicken as part of a cold buffet.

Serves 4

450g, 1lb cooked chicken, sliced
100g, 4oz seedless green grapes, halved
mixed salad leaves
150ml, ¼pt (²/₃ cup) olive oil
2 tsp caster sugar
2 tsp mustard
1 tbsp white wine vinegar
2 tbsp clear honey
grated rind and juice of 1 small lemon
chopped fresh herbs - thyme, basil, marjoram, hyssop,
tarragon, mint and parsley or a combination of these

Arrange the chicken slices and grapes over a bed of mixed salad leaves. Make up the herby dressing by combining the olive oil, sugar, mustard, vinegar, honey, lemon and herbs. Pour over the chicken and serve.

BARBECUED TURKEY KEBABS

Serves 4

450g, 1lb turkey breast, cut into strips
grated rind and juice of 1 lemon
1 tbsp soya sauce
1 tbsp clear honey
4 tbsp olive oil
2 tbsp chopped mint

Heat together the lemon juice, rind, soya sauce, honey, oil and mint. Pour this marinade over the turkey strips in a dish and leave for at least 2 hours. Thread the turkey onto skewers and place over a barbecue. Brush with the marinade and barbecue until well cooked.

SPICY TURKEY AND NOODLES

Serves 4

450g, 1lb skinless turkey breast
1 tsp caster sugar
½ tsp each of salt, pepper, ground ginger
mustard powder, turmeric and curry powder
325g, 12oz courgette
125g, 5oz mange tout
1 red pepper
1 yellow pepper
4 tbsp olive oil
2 tbsp clear honey
4 tbsp lemon juice
1 tbsp soya sauce
250g, 9oz medium egg noodles

Cut the turkey into strips and mix with the sugar, salt, pepper, ginger, mustard powder, turmeric and curry powder. Chill overnight. Slice the courgettes, cut the peppers into strips and sauté the mange tout, courgettes and peppers for a few minutes. Sauté the turkey and then stir in the honey, lemon juice and soya sauce. Cover the pan and simmer for a further few minutes until the turkey is tender. Cook the noodles and mix with the turkey and vegetables. Serve warm or cold.

DUCK WITH HONEY
AND GRAPE SAUCE

Serves 4

4 portions of duck
salt
4 tbsp clear honey
grated rind and juice of half an orange
225g, 8oz green seedless grapes
14g, ½oz (1 tbsp) butter

Prick the portions of duck and rub salt into them. Place in a roasting dish and cook in the oven at gas mark 4, 180°C (350°F) for 1½ hours. Heat the honey, orange rind and juice, grapes and butter and bring to the boil. Pour over the duck portions and return to the oven for another 5 minutes.

PERSIAN DUCK BREASTS

Serves 4

4 boned duck breasts
juice of 1 lemon
1 tbsp honey
4 pomegranates
salt and pepper
1 tbsp olive oil
1 onion, peeled and finely chopped
50g, 2oz (½ cup) walnuts, chopped

Halve the pomegranates and put the seeds into a food processor. Process and then pass through a sieve. Pour this juice, the lemon juice, honey, a little extra water and a pinch of salt and pepper into a saucepan and bring to the boil. Simmer for 20 minutes and then cool. Prepare the duck breasts by scoring the fat with diagonal cuts. Pour the pomegranate mixture over the duck breasts and allow to marinate for a few hours. Grill the breasts under a hot grill until well browned on both sides. In a pan fry the onions and walnuts in the oil for a few minutes and add the pomegranate marinade. Simmer for a few minutes and then serve the breasts with some of the sauce poured over each one.

VENISON STEAKS WITH HONEY AND YOGHURT SAUCE

These steaks are delicious with mange tout or French beans
and new potatoes.

Serves 2

2 venison steaks
salt and pepper
1 tbsp sunflower oil
1 tsp honey
2 tbsp yoghurt
2 tsp green peppercorns
100g, 4oz mushrooms, sliced

Season the steaks with salt and pepper. Fry the steaks in the
oil until tender. Remove from the pan and cut into slices. Fry
the sliced mushrooms in the same pan and then add the honey,
yoghurt and peppercorns and stir into the juices. Heat for a
couple of minutes and pour over the steaks.

GAMMON WITH HONEY GLAZE

This is the traditional way of serving the rind from a gammon joint.

Serves 6 - 8

1 joint of boiled gammon

Glaze

1 tbsp honey
50g, 2oz (½ cup) brown sugar
juice of 1 lemon
1 tsp mustard

Cut the rind off the gammon and score the fat into diamond shapes. Put the rind in a roasting tin. Blend together the honey, sugar, lemon juice and mustard and smear all over the rind. Roast in the oven at gas mark 6, 200°C (400°F) for 15 minutes. Cool and serve sliced with the gammon.

SWEET AND SOUR BACON SLICES

These bacon slices are tangy and delicious. Serve with potatoes and spinach.

Serves 2

2 bacon slices
3 tbsp pineapple juice
2 tbsp dry white wine
2 tsp lemon juice
1 tbsp honey
2 tsp Worcestershire sauce
1 tsp cornflour
1 tsp ginger
pineapple rings to garnish

Put the bacon slices into a baking dish. Mix all the other ingredients together and pour over the slices. Cover and cook in the oven at gas mark 4, 180°C (350°F) for 30 minutes, basting and turning the slices over half way through the cooking time. Serve garnished with pineapple rings.

PORK CHOPS WITH HONEY AND CIDER

I love the sauce that comes with these pork chops. Serve with rice and green vegetables.

Serves 4

4 pork chops
25g, 1oz (2 tbsp) butter
1 tbsp sunflower oil
2 onions, peeled and sliced
1 clove of garlic, peeled and crushed
2 cooking apples, peeled, cored and sliced
½ tsp dried thyme
1 tbsp clear honey
240ml, 8fl oz (1 cup) sweet cider
1 tbsp brandy
4 tbsp cream
parsley for garnish

Brown the chops in the oil and butter in a frying pan and transfer to a casserole. Fry the onions and garlic and add to the casserole. Soften the apple slices in the frying pan, cooking them for a couple of minutes. Stir them into the casserole. Add the thyme, honey, cider, and brandy. Cover and cook for 40 minutes in the oven at gas mark 4, 180°C (350°F). Skim off any fat that has risen to the surface and stir in the cream. Serve at once garnished with parsley.

BARBECUED SPARE RIBS

Serves 4 - 6

900g, 2lb spare ribs of pork
2 tbsp tomato purée
4 tbsp soya sauce
2 tbsp honey
2 cloves of garlic, peeled and crushed
1 onion, peeled and chopped
2 tsp mustard

Lay the spare ribs in an ovenproof dish. Mix the tomato purée, soya sauce, honey, garlic and onion together and brush over the meat. Barbecue or put in the oven at gas mark 5, 190°C (375°F) for 1 hour. Turn the meat over half way through the cooking time.

SWEET AND SOUR MEATBALLS

Serve these meatballs with rice or noodles and green beans.

Serves 4

450g, 1lb minced pork
1 onion, peeled and chopped
1 tbsp sunflower oil
1 small red pepper
1 small green pepper
1 small yellow pepper
1 tbsp red wine vinegar
1 tbsp honey
1 tsp soya sauce
5 tbsp orange juice
5 tbsp chicken stock
pinch of ground ginger
2 tsp cornflour
salt and pepper

Mix the pork, onion, salt and pepper together and shape into balls. Fry in the sunflower oil in a frying pan. Place in a serving dish and keep warm. Slice the peppers and fry in the pan for 5 minutes. Add the vinegar, honey, soya sauce, orange juice, chicken stock and ground ginger. Stir everything together and cook for 15 minutes. Mix the cornflour with a little cold water and stir into the sauce. Pour over the meat balls and serve.

COD IN
SWEET AND SOUR SAUCE

This is an unusual sauce for cod but it is delicious and very
quick and easy.

Serves 4

A small bunch of spring onions, chopped
4 cod steaks
a little sunflower oil
1 tbsp tomato purée
1 tbsp soya sauce
1 tbsp honey
1 tbsp dry sherry
juice of 1 orange
pinch of cayenne pepper
1 carrot, cut into chunks

Brush cod steaks with oil and grill for 5 minutes on each side.
Mix all the remaining ingredients and simmer until thickened a
little. Put the cod in a serving dish and pour over the sauce.

HONEY GRILLED TROUT

Serves 4

4 rainbow trout, gutted and cleaned
75g, 3oz ($^1/_3$ cup) butter
1 tbsp chopped parsley
2 tbsp clear honey
2 tbsp lemon juice

Use a sharp knife to make diagonal slashes on the sides of the
trout. Cream half the butter with the parsley and put inside
each trout. Put the rest of the butter, honey and lemon juice in
a saucepan and heat gently. Pour over the trout. Cook the
trout in a grill pan under a hot grill for 10 minutes on each side.
Serve with the juices from the pan.

SALMON WITH
LIME AND HONEY

Serves 4

4 salmon steaks
grated rind and juice of 1 lime
5 tbsp sunflower oil
2 tbsp orange juice
2 tsp honey
1 green cardamom, crushed to extract seeds

Whisk together 3 tablespoons of oil, lime rind and juice, orange juice, honey and crushed cardamom seeds. Marinade the salmon steaks in this mixture overnight. Take the salmon out of the marinade and brush with the remaining oil. Grill, turning the steaks for about 8 minutes. Pour the marinade into a saucepan and bring to the boil. Serve the salmon steaks with the warm sauce.

VEGETABLES AND SALADS

Glazed Carrots

Roast Potatoes with Honey and Sesame Seeds

Parsnips with Honey

Honey Glazed Onions

Stir Fry Veggies

Spiced Red Cabbage

Sweetcorn Salad

Beetroot Salad

GLAZED CARROTS

Serves 4

450g, 1lb carrots, peeled and chopped
1 tbsp honey
3 tbsp water
1 tbsp butter
1 tbsp parsley

Put the honey and water in a saucepan, add the carrots and cook for 8 minutes. Drain but leave a little liquid in the saucepan. Add the butter and heat gently. Stir the carrots in the butter and serve with the parsley.

ROAST POTATOES WITH HONEY AND SESAME SEEDS

Prepare your usual quantity of potatoes for roasting. Put into a roasting tin and drizzle with olive oil. Cook in the oven at gas mark 5, 190°C (375°F) for 30 minutes. Remove from the oven, drizzle with some honey and sprinkle with sesame seeds. Return to the oven for another 30 minutes.

PARSNIPS WITH HONEY

Serves 4

450g, 1lb parsnips, peeled and chopped
2 tbsp wholegrain mustard
2 tbsp honey
150ml, ¼ pt (²/₃ cup) orange juice
150ml, ¼pt (²/₃ cup) chicken stock

Mix together the mustard and honey and stir in the orange juice and stock. Put the parsnips in a dish and pour over the sauce. Cover with silver foil or a lid and cook in the oven at gas mark 4, 180°C (350°F) for 30 minutes. Then remove the foil or lid and cook for another 10 minutes to brown the parsnips.

HONEY GLAZED ONIONS

These delicious onions go well with pork, gammon or sausages.

Serves 4

450g, 1lb onions, peeled
25g, 1oz (1 tbsp) butter
1 tbsp clear honey
1 tbsp sugar
juice of ½ lemon
½ tsp Worcestershire sauce
½ tsp white wine vinegar
salt and pepper

Cover the onions with cold water and bring to the boil. Simmer for 5 minutes to blanch them and then drain. Melt the butter in a saucepan, add the honey, sugar, lemon juice, Worcestershire sauce, vinegar and salt and pepper. Stir over a low heat until everything is blended. Add the onions, cover with a lid and simmer gently for 20 minutes. Uncover towards the end of the cooking time to help the onions to glaze to a golden colour. Serve hot with the juices from the pan.

STIR FRY VEGGIES

This is delicious as part of a vegetarian meal or as a vegetable side dish served with chicken and rice.

Serves 4

225g, 8oz broccoli
4 spring onions
1 red pepper
1 yellow pepper
1 courgette
2 tbsp sunflower oil
1 piece root ginger, grated

Sauce

3 tbsp dry sherry
1 tbsp soya sauce
1 tsp caster sugar
1 tbsp clear honey
½ tsp ground ginger
1 tbsp tomato purée
1 tbsp cornflour

Chop the vegetables into bite size pieces. Mix the sauce ingredients together to make a smooth paste. Heat the oil in a wok and add the onions first with the ginger. Stir fry for a couple of minutes, then add the peppers, courgette and broccoli and continue to stir fry for a few minutes. Stir in the sauce and bring to the boil. Serve steaming hot.

SPICED RED CABBAGE

Serves 4

450g, 1lb red cabbage
25g, 1oz (1 tbsp) butter
1 small onion, peeled and chopped
225g, 8oz eating apples, peeled, cored and chopped
150ml, ¼pt (²/₃ cup) water
2 tbsp wine vinegar
1 tbsp honey
pinch of nutmeg
salt and pepper

Shred the red cabbage. Fry the onion in the butter in a casserole or large saucepan and add the apples. After a couple of minutes add the red cabbage. Mix in the water, vinegar and honey and season with the nutmeg, salt and pepper. Cover and cook on a low heat for about 30 minutes. Top up with more water if the cabbage becomes too dry.

SWEETCORN SALAD

Serves 4

4 tbsp sunflower oil
1 tbsp honey
1 tbsp tomato ketchup
1 tbsp Worcestershire sauce
1 tbsp grated onion
50g, 2oz raisins
450g, 1lb sweetcorn kernels, canned and drained
1 red pepper, chopped
1 green pepper, chopped

Pour the oil, vinegar, Worcestershire sauce, tomato ketchup, honey and grated onion into a bowl and mix well. Stir in the raisins, sweetcorn and chopped peppers.

BEETROOT SALAD

Serves 2 - 4

225g, 8oz beetroot, diced
1 orange, peeled and sliced
1 pear, peeled and sliced
90ml, 3fl oz (¹/₃ cup) Greek yoghurt
1 tbsp honey
1 tbsp lemon juice
4 tsp chopped chives
lettuce leaves for garnish

Mix together the beetroot, pear and orange. Make the dressing by mixing honey, lemon juice, chives and yoghurt together. Mix this into the beetroot and fruit mixture. Arrange the salad on the lettuce leaves and serve at once.

DRESSINGS AND
SAVOURY SAUCES

Paprika Dressing

Honey and Lemon Dressing

Chive, Ginger and Honey Dressing

Yoghurt Mayonnaise

Honey and Orange Mayonnaise

Home-made Mustard

Horseradish Sauce

Barbecue Sauce

PAPRIKA DRESSING

1 tbsp clear honey
½ tsp salt
1 tbsp water
2 tsp paprika
1 tbsp Dijon mustard
sprinkling of pepper
150ml, ¼pt (²/₃ cup) olive oil
60ml, 2fl oz (¼ cup) red wine vinegar

Put the honey, salt and water in a jar, screw the lid on and shake until well mixed. Add the paprika, mustard and pepper. Shake again. Add the oil and vinegar and shake once more.

HONEY AND LEMON DRESSING

180ml, 6fl oz (¾ cup) sunflower oil
60ml, 2fl oz (¼ cup) lemon juice
60ml, 2fl oz (¼ cup) clear honey
1 tsp grated onion
¼ tsp mustard powder
1 tsp paprika

Combine all the ingredients in a bowl and whisk together. Use straight away.

CHIVE, GINGER AND HONEY DRESSING

2 tsp ginger
5 tbsp lemon juice
2 tbsp clear honey
2 tbsp soya sauce
4 tbsp chopped chives

Mix all the ingredients together well and pour over the salad of your choice.

YOGHURT MAYONNAISE

120ml, 4fl oz (½ cup) plain yoghurt
1 tbsp clear honey
1 tsp lemon juice
90ml, 3fl oz (⅓ cup) mayonnaise
1 tsp poppy seeds
pinch of salt

Combine the yoghurt, honey and lemon juice and stir. Add the mayonnaise, salt and poppy seeds. Chill and serve.

HONEY AND ORANGE
MAYONNAISE

240ml, 8fl oz (1 cup) mayonnaise
150g, 6oz (½ cup) clear honey
1 tbsp orange juice
1 tbsp grated lemon rind

Place the mayonnaise and honey in a bowl. Mix well and add the orange juice and lemon rind. This is quite a strong tasting dressing for salads so it should be used sparingly. It can also be used as a dip for fruits.

HOME-MADE MUSTARD

1kg, 2.2lb mustard seeds
2 tbsp clear honey
enough cider vinegar to cover the seeds
salt
pinch of turmeric
pinch of cayenne pepper

Put the mustard seeds into a large bowl and add the honey, turmeric and cayenne pepper. Fill the bowl with the cider vinegar so that it just covers the seeds. Leave for three days covered with cling film. Stir the mixture every so often. Pour into jars and seal well.

HORSERADISH SAUCE

2 tbsp grated horseradish
1 tbsp white wine vinegar
½ tsp dry mustard
1 tsp honey
salt and pepper
150ml, ¼pt (²/₃ cup) whipped cream

Mix together the horseradish, honey and mustard. Fold in the cream. Add the vinegar, salt and pepper and mix everything together.

BARBECUE SAUCE

1 clove of garlic, peeled and crushed
1 tsp paprika
pinch of chilli powder
4 tbsp honey
3 tbsp tomato purée
4 tbsp orange juice
4 tbsp wine vinegar
3 tbsp soya sauce
1 tbsp Worcestershire sauce

Mix all the ingredients together and simmer for 5 minutes. Serve with any barbecued or grilled meats.

PUDDINGS

Creamy Desserts

Honey Mousse

Honey Rice Pudding

Atholl Brose

Alternative Atholl Brose

Toffee Crunch Honey Pudding

Chocolate and Muesli Pudding

Honeycomb Mould

Easy Honey Cream

Honey and Brandy Cream

Apple and Mint Whip

Crunchy Apple Whip

Banana and Honey Yoghurt

Honey Soufflé

Honey Crème Caramel

White Chocolate Mousse

Lemon Syllabub

Chocolate and Chestnut Cream

Italian Ricotta Dessert

Honey and Lemon Semolina

HONEY MOUSSE

This mousse goes well with summer fruits such as raspberries, strawberries or blackcurrants.

3 eggs, separated
100g, 4oz (²/₃ cup) caster sugar
grated rind and juice of 2 lemons
2 tsp gelatine or vege-gel (the vegetarian equivalent)
150ml, ¼pt (²/₃ cup) whipped cream
2 tbsp honey

Put the egg yolks, sugar, lemon rind and juice in a bowl and whisk over a pan of simmering water until thick. Remove from the heat and continue to whisk until cool. Soak the gelatine in the juice from the other lemon and stir over a pan of hot water until dissolved. Whisk the egg whites until stiff. Fold the whipped cream into the mousse with the gelatine, honey and whisked egg whites. Chill until ready to serve.

HONEY RICE PUDDING

All the family will love this rice pudding.

600ml, 1pt (2½ cups) milk
300ml, ½pt (1¼ cups) carton single cream
75g, 3oz (½ cup) pudding rice
knob of butter
2 tbsp caster sugar
few drops vanilla essence
pinch of nutmeg
2 tbsp clear honey
1 tbsp lemon juice

Mix together all the ingredients except the honey and lemon juice. Pour into an ovenproof dish and cook in a cool oven, gas mark 2, 150°C (300°F) for about three hours. Stir in any skin that forms. Mix together the honey and lemon juice and drizzle over the rice pudding. Place under a hot grill until golden brown.

ATHOLL BROSE

This is a version of the traditional Scottish pudding.

600ml, 1pt (2½ cups) double cream
5 tbsp whisky
3 tbsp clear honey
50g, 2oz (½ cup) oatmeal

Whip the double cream until thick and then gradually add the whisky, while continuing to whip the cream. Stir in the honey. Toast the oatmeal by shaking it around in a saucepan over a moderate heat. Cool the oatmeal before stirring it into the whisky and honey cream. Serve in individual glasses.

ALTERNATIVE ATHOLL BROSE

6 tbsp whisky
4 tbsp lemon juice
4 tbsp clear honey
600ml, 1pt (2½ cups) double cream
75g, 3oz (¾ cup) ground almonds
100g, 4oz (1¾ cups) porridge oats, browned under the grill

Mix the whisky with the lemon juice and honey in a bowl. Add the cream and whisk until thick but don't overdo it. Gently fold in the ground almonds and the toasted oats.

TOFFEE CRUNCH
HONEY PUDDING

600ml, 1pt (2½ cups) double cream
150ml, ¼pt (²/₃ cup) whisky
2 tbsp honey

Topping

50g, 2oz (¼ cup) butter
50g, 2oz (½ cup) brown sugar
3 tbsp golden syrup
100g, 4oz (1¾ cups) oats

Whip the cream. Fold in the whisky and honey. For the topping, melt the butter, sugar and syrup until the sugar has dissolved. Boil for 2 minutes and then stir in the oats and cook for another minute. Cool and just before serving cover the cream with the oat mixture.

CHOCOLATE AND
MUESLI PUDDING

1 large carton Greek yoghurt
50g, 2oz (1 cup) muesli base
50g, 2oz (½ cup) hazelnuts
150g, 6oz dried apple rings
2 tbsp honey
100g , 4oz plain chocolate
25g, 1oz (2 tbsp) butter

Stir the muesli and hazelnuts into the yoghurt. Stir in the honey and dried apple rings. Melt the chocolate with the butter over a pan of simmering water. Stir until smooth and then layer the yoghurt mixture with the chocolate either in individual glasses or in a bowl.

HONEYCOMB MOULD

This is delicious served with strawberries or raspberries.

600ml, 1pt (2½ cups) single cream
2 eggs, separated
2 tbsp clear honey
14g, ½oz gelatine or vege-gel (the vegetarian
equivalent)
¼ tsp vanilla essence
2 tbsp warm water

Heat the cream until it is just below boiling point. Beat together the egg yolks and honey until thick. Gradually pour on the heated cream and continue to whisk over a pan of simmering water, until the mixture thickens. Stir in the vanilla essence. Dissolve the gelatine in the water and pour carefully into the cream mixture and stir together. Whisk the egg whites and fold into the mixture. Pour the whole mixture into a mould or bowl and refrigerate for a few hours before turning out. Serve with summer fruits.

EASY HONEY CREAM

This goes well with summer fruits.

3 eggs
3 tbsp clear honey
240ml, 8fl oz (1 cup) whipping cream
2 tbsp sherry
2 tbsp chopped Brazil nuts

Whisk together the egg yolks and honey over a bowl of simmering water. Whisk the egg whites and whisk the cream in a separate bowl. Gradually stir the cream into the egg yolk mixture and add the sherry. Fold in the whisked egg whites. Serve in individual glasses and sprinkle with the nuts.

HONEY AND BRANDY CREAM

150ml, ¼pt (²/₃ cup) double cream
2 tbsp clear honey
1 tbsp brandy
1 egg white
ground cinnamon

Whip the cream and then trickle in the honey and brandy. Continue whipping until thick. Chill. Whisk the egg white and fold into the cream mixture. Serve dusted with cinnamon.

APPLE AND MINT WHIP

The apple combined with mint gives a lovely flavour to this
light dessert.

450g, 1lb cooking apples, peeled, cored and chopped
1 tbsp fresh mint leaves
3 tbsp clear honey
2 egg whites
1 tbsp brown sugar
5 tbsp Greek yoghurt

Cook the apples gently in a covered saucepan with the honey
and mint. If the apples start to stick to the bottom of the saucepan you may have to add a little water. When cooked reduce
to a purée, having discarded the mint. Mix the sugar into the
yoghurt and fold into the apple purée. Whisk the egg whites
and fold them into the apple and yoghurt mixture. Chill until
ready to serve and garnish with some more mint leaves if liked.

CRUNCHY APPLE WHIP

100g, 4oz ginger biscuits, crushed
50g, 2oz (½ cup) ground hazelnuts
450g, 1lb cooking apples, cored, peeled and sliced
3 tbsp honey
rind and juice of 1 lemon
1 egg white
25g, 1oz (1tbsp) sugar
150ml, ¼pt (²/₃ cup) whipped cream

Stir the crushed biscuits and hazelnuts together. Put the honey, lemon rind, juice and apples in a saucepan, and cook until tender. Mix up to a purée. Whisk the egg white and whisk in the sugar. Fold this mixture and the apple mixture into the cream. Spoon some of the apple mixture into a serving bowl. Cover with a layer of biscuit crumbs. Repeat the layers, finishing with a layer of biscuit.

BANANA AND
HONEY YOGHURT

A very simple pudding which is healthy and nutritious.

300ml, ½pt (1¼ cups) natural yoghurt
2 bananas
1 tsp brown sugar
1 tbsp clear honey

Mash the bananas and add to the yoghurt with the honey and sugar. Mix well and chill for at least an hour to allow the flavours to develop.

HONEY SOUFFLÉ

This cold souffle is nice with sliced fruit such as bananas, grapes or kiwi fruit.

3 large eggs, separated
2 tbsp well-flavoured honey
juice of ½ lemon
150ml, ¼pt (²/₃ cup) double cream

Add the honey and lemon juice to the egg yolks in a bowl and whisk over a pan of simmering water until thick and creamy. Whip the cream until thick and stir into the honey mixture. Whisk the egg whites and fold them in too. Chill in a bowl in the fridge and then serve.

HONEY CRÈME CARAMEL

3 eggs and 1 egg yolk
1 tbsp honey
450ml, ¾pt (1¾ cups) milk
a pinch of nutmeg

Beat the eggs and egg yolk with the honey. Pour on the milk and strain into an ovenproof dish. Sprinkle on the nutmeg. Stand the dish in a roasting tin half full of water. Put in the oven at gas mark 4, 180°C (350°F) for about an hour until the custard is cooked.

WHITE CHOCOLATE MOUSSE

This mousse goes well with a fudge or chocolate sauce or
with summer fruits.

2 tbsp clear honey
1 tsp gelatine or vege-gel (the vegetarian equivalent)
7 tbsp cold water
325g, 12oz white chocolate
3 egg yolks
350ml, 12fl oz (1½ cups) whipped cream

Dissolve the gelatine in 2 tablespoons of the water over a low
heat. Mix the other 5 tablespoons of water with the honey and
bring to the boil. Remove from the heat and stir in the white
chocolate, and the gelatine. Then stir in the egg yolks and fold
in the whipped cream. Pour the whole mixture into a serving
bowl and chill in the fridge, preferably over-night.

LEMON SYLLABUB

This is a honey version of the traditional syllabub made with sugar.

grated rind and juice of 1 lemon
1 tbsp brandy
1 tbsp sherry
240ml, 8fl oz (1 cup) milk
300ml, ½pt (1¼ cups) double cream
2 tbsp honey

Mix the lemon rind and juice, brandy and sherry together and leave for an hour. Add the other ingredients and whisk together until thick. Spoon into individual gasses or serve in one glass bowl.

CHOCOLATE AND
CHESTNUT CREAM

This is a lovely rich pudding. You can serve it in individual ramekin dishes and it would serve 8 at a dinner party.

150g, 6oz plain chocolate
75g, 3oz (¹/₃ cup) butter
75g, 3oz (¼ cup) honey
1 can of sweetened chestnut purée
3 tbsp brandy
300ml, ½pt (1¼ cups) double cream

Melt the chocolate in a bowl over a pan of simmering water. Cream the butter and honey and mix in the chestnut purée. Add the melted chocolate, the brandy and the cream. Leave in the fridge to set.

ITALIAN RICOTTA DESSERT

300g, 11oz (1½ cups) ricotta
3 eggs
100g, 4oz (1cup) almonds
few drops of almond essence
325g, 12oz (1 cup) well-flavoured honey
2 tbsp breadcrumbs
juice of 1 orange

Process or blend the ricotta. Add the almonds, almond essence, 150g, 6oz (½ cup) of the honey and the eggs. Grease a 20cm (8in) flan dish and sprinkle the breadcrumbs on it. Pour in the ricotta mixture and bake at gas mark 6, 200°C (400°F) for about 40 minutes. Mix the orange juice and remaining honey together and pour over the pudding. Chill overnight.

HONEY AND LEMON SEMOLINA

Children will enjoy this pudding especially if you serve a little
Ribena with it.

600ml, 1pt (2½ cups) milk
2 tbsp honey
75g, 3oz (¾ cup) semolina
25g, 1oz (1 tbsp) butter
grated rind and juice of 1 lemon
1 tsp cinnamon
2 eggs, beaten

Whisk the milk, honey, semolina, butter, grated lemon rind and
cinnamon together in a pan over a gentle heat until the mixture
thickens and simmer for 5 minutes. Pour the mixture over the
eggs and continue whisking, in a bowl over a pan of simmering
water for a couple of minutes. Remove from the heat, and add
the lemon juice. Chill before serving.

Fruity Desserts

Poached Peaches with Mascarpone
Stuffed Peaches in Honey Syrup
Nectarine and Plum Pizzetta
Raspberry Crumble
Raspberry Sponge Pudding
Blackcurrant Kissel
Blackcurrant and Honey Ambrosia
Blackcurrant and Ricotta Dessert
Strawberry and Lemon Tipsy Trifle
Honey-Glazed Savarin with Strawberries
Summer Fruit Salad
Winter Fruit Salad
Pineapple in Honey Syrup
Pears with Cream and Honey
Plums with Port
Kiwi Syllabub
Lemon Whip with Grapes
Rhubarb Fool
Gooseberry Fool
Pear and Honey Pancakes
Orange and Lemon Pancakes
Baked Figs with Mascarpone and Hazelnuts
Grapefruit and Honey Layered Pudding
Poached Apricots
Baked Honey Apples
Honey and Blackberry Upside Down Pudding

POACHED PEACHES
WITH MASCARPONE

This is a delicious way to serves peaches.

300ml, ½pt (1½ cups) white wine
4 tbsp well flavoured honey
4 large peaches
225g, 8oz (1 cup) mascarpone
2 tbsp icing sugar
sprinkling of demerara sugar

Put the wine and honey in a saucepan and heat to dissolve. Skin and halve the peaches, remove the stones and cut them into quarters.If you put the peaches in boiling water for a few seconds you will find the skins will come off more easily. Add the peaches to the pan, cover and heat them gently for 20 minutes. Remove and put in a dish. Bring the syrup in the pan to the boil and cook to reduce and thicken it. Pour over the peaches. Beat the mascarpone with the icing sugar and spoon over the peaches. Sprinkle with the demerara sugar and put under the grill for a couple of minutes. Serve straight away.

STUFFED PEACHES
IN HONEY SYRUP

4 peaches

Filling

75g, 3oz (¾ cup) ground almonds
50g, 2oz (¼ cup) sponge cake crumbs
1 egg yolk

Syrup

4 tbsp honey
5 tbsp water
juice of 1 orange

Skin and halve the peaches. If you put the peaches in boiling water for a few seconds you will find the skins will come off more easily. Remove the stones. Mix the almonds, cake crumbs and egg yolk together and fill each peach half with the mixture. Make the syrup by warming the honey, water and orange juice together. Place the peaches in a buttered ovenproof dish and pour the syrup over them. Bake in the oven at gas mark 4, 180°C (350°F) for about 30 minutes.

NECTARINE AND PLUM PIZZETTA

This is a great idea for using up left over nectarines.

325g, 12oz puff pastry
2 tbsp apricot jam
4 nectarines, de-stoned
3 plums, de-stoned
50g, 2oz (¼ cup) butter, melted
2 tbsp honey
1 egg yolk

Roll out the pastry and line a greased Swiss roll tin with it. Spread the apricot jam over the pastry. Slice the nectarines and plums and arrange neatly over the pastry. Brush with butter and dribble honey over the fruit. Brush the pastry edges with beaten egg yolk. Cook in the oven at gas mark 4, 180°C (350°F) for 30 minutes. Make sure the puff pastry is cooked before removing it from the oven. Cut into squares and serve with ice-cream.

RASPBERRY CRUMBLE

This is a simple but yummy crumble and will be enjoyed by all the family.

225g, 8oz cooking apples, peeled, cored and sliced
225g, 8oz raspberries
3 tbsp clear honey

Crumble topping

150g, 6oz (1½ cups) plain wholemeal flour
75g, 3oz (⅓ cup) margarine
50g, 2oz (½ cup) brown sugar

Mix the apples with the raspberries and put them into a baking dish. Spoon the honey over them. Rub the margarine into the flour until the mixture is like breadcrumbs and stir in the sugar. Sprinkle the crumble topping over the apple and raspberry mixture. Bake in the oven at gas mark 4, 180°C (350°F) for 40 minutes.

RASPBERRY SPONGE PUDDING

This is very tasty although not a particularly elegant pudding.

450g, 1lb raspberries
50g, 2oz (¼ cup) butter
5 tbsp honey
225g, 8oz (2 cups) sponge cake broken up into pieces
2 eggs, beaten

Cook the raspberries for a few minutes. Add the butter and honey and allow the butter to melt. Remove from the heat and add the sponge and beaten eggs. Mix everything together, pour into a 27.5 x 17.5cm (11 x 7in) ovenproof dish and bake in the oven at gas mark 4, 180°C (350°F) for about 35 minutes.

BLACKCURRANT KISSEL

This pudding is quite runny and has the consistency of a thick soup. It goes really well with ice-cream, and in particular with the mascarpone and honey ice-cream (see page 117). It could also be served as a topping poured onto a sponge pudding or onto rice pudding.

450g, 1lb blackcurrants
3 tbsp clear honey
juice of 1 lemon
pinch of nutmeg
1 - 2 tbsp caster sugar
25g, 1oz (¼ cup) wholemeal flour

Put the blackcurrants, honey and lemon juice into a saucepan with enough cold water just to cover the fruit. Heat gently and simmer until the fruit is soft. Sieve the fruit, and add a pinch of nutmeg. At this stage taste the purée. If it is too tart add 1 or 2 tablespoons of caster sugar. Put the flour into a bowl and stir in some of the blackcurrant mixture to make a paste. Mix this paste into the rest of the purée and stir over a low heat until thickened. Cool before serving.

BLACKCURRANT AND
HONEY AMBROSIA

This is delicious and a particularly healthy dessert for the
children as it is full of vitamin C. It is also a wonderful
reddish purple colour.

100g, 4oz blackcurrants
100g, 4oz redcurrants
50g, 2oz ($^1/_3$ cup) sugar
50g, 2oz ($^1/_3$ cup) medium oatmeal
300ml, ½pt (1¼ cups) double cream
4 tbsp clear honey

Cook the black and redcurrants together with the sugar, adding a little water until they are soft. Sieve this mixture to remove
the pips. Toast the oatmeal in the oven or under the grill and
then allow to cool. Whip the cream and stir in the black and
redcurrant purée, oatmeal, and honey.

BLACKCURRANT AND RICOTTA DESSERT

This is another healthy dessert.

225g, 8oz blackcurrants
50g, 2oz (¹/₃ cup) sugar
1 tsp cornflour
100g, 4oz (1 cup) ricotta
1 small carton Greek yoghurt
2 tbsp honey

Cook the blackcurrants in a saucepan with the sugar and a tablespoon of water for about 10 minutes. Mix the cornflour to a paste with a few drops of water and blend into the blackcurrant mixture. Cook for a couple more minutes. Beat together the ricotta, Greek yoghurt and honey and place in a serving bowl. Pour the blackcurrant mixture over the top and blend in to give a marbled effect. Serve at once.

STRAWBERRY AND LEMON
TIPSY TRIFLE

If you feel like indulging, here is a delicious version of a trifle.

450g, 1lb strawberries, hulled and quartered
100g, 4oz ratafia biscuits
90ml, 3fl oz ($^1/_3$ cup) sweet wine
3 tbsp honey
2 tbsp brandy
juice of 1 lemon
150ml, ¼pt ($^2/_3$ cup) double cream
2 egg whites

Mix the strawberries with the biscuits and put in a large glass bowl. Pour 2 tablespoons of the wine over them. Mix together the remaining wine, honey, brandy and 3 tablespoons of lemon juice. Whip the cream and gradually whisk into the wine mixture. Whisk the egg whites and fold into the cream mixture. Pour over the strawberries. Cover and chill for an hour before serving.

HONEY-GLAZED SAVARIN
WITH STRAWBERRIES

325g, 12oz (3 cups) flour
1 sachet fast acting yeast
½ tsp salt
3 tbsp caster sugar
90ml, 3fl oz (⅓ cup) milk
150g, 6oz (¾ cup) butter
6 eggs
450g, 1lb strawberries, hulled and halved

Syrup

600ml, 1pt (2½ cups) cider
6 tbsp clear honey

Mix the yeast into the flour and add the salt and caster sugar. Add the milk, butter and eggs and beat together well. Turn the mixture into a greased savarin or ring mould, cover with a damp tea-towel and leave in a warm room to rise for about 30 minutes. Bake in the oven at gas mark 6, 200°C (400°F) for 20 minutes. To make the syrup, heat the cider and boil until reduced by half. Then stir in the honey and cool. Turn out the savarin and pour over the cider syrup. Fill the centre with the strawberries.

SUMMER FRUIT SALAD

This is an easy but delicious healthy fruit salad. Serve with cream unless you are watching the calories, in which case serve with fromage frais or yoghurt.

3 nectarines
225g, 8oz strawberries, sliced
100g, 4oz redcurrants
100g, 4oz blackcurrants
300ml, ½pt (1¼ cups) red grape juice
2 tbsp clear honey

Cut the nectarines in half and remove the stones. Chop them up and put into a bowl with the sliced strawberries, blackcurrants and redcurrants. Mix the honey and grape juice together and pour over the fruit. Chill for at least 30 minutes before serving to allow the flavours to be absorbed.

WINTER FRUIT SALAD

2 bananas
2 Cox's eating apples
2 oranges
100g, 4oz seedless green grapes
1 grapefruit
3 tbsp clear honey
1 tbsp of lemon juice

Cut all the fruit up, except the bananas and arrange in a bowl. Add the honey and lemon juice. Leave to stand for at least an hour. The honey will draw out the juices and make a syrup. Slice the bananas into the fruit salad just before serving.

PINEAPPLE IN HONEY SYRUP

1 pineapple, peeled and sliced into rings
juice of 1 lemon
2 tbsp clear honey
2 tbsp Marsala
25g, 1oz (2tbsp) butter
90ml, 3fl oz ($^1/_3$ cup) single cream

Marinade the pineapple rings in 1 tablespoon of the honey, the Marsala and the lemon juice overnight. Drain the pineapple rings and fry in the butter without letting them colour. Pour the reserved marinade into a saucepan and add a little water and the remaining honey. Heat gently and add the single cream. Pour over the pineapple rings and serve.

PEARS WITH CREAM AND HONEY

4 pears, peeled and cored
50g, 2oz (¼ cup) butter
150ml, ¼pt (²/₃ cup) cream
1 tbsp set honey

Slice the pears and fry them in the butter for a few minutes. Turn into an ovenproof dish. Pour over the cream and honey and bake in the oven at gas mark 4, 180°C (350°F) for 15 minutes.

PLUMS WITH PORT

A healthy dessert and the port gives it extra flavour.

450g, 1lb plums
120ml, 4fl oz (½ cup) apple juice
1 tbsp clear honey
2 tbsp port
3 tbsp Greek yoghurt

Halve and stone the plums and cook with the honey and apple juice in a saucepan over a gentle heat for about 15 minutes until the plums are soft. Mix in the port and then add the Greek yoghurt and mix gently to give a marbled effect.

KIWI SYLLABUB

A quick and delicious dessert.

300ml, ½pt (1¼ cups) double cream
2 tbsp brandy
1 tbsp honey
6 kiwi fruit, peeled and sliced

Whip the cream until stiff and whip in the brandy and honey. Pour into a serving dish and top with the kiwi fruit.

LEMON WHIP WITH GRAPES

150ml, ¼pt (²/₃ cup) Greek yoghurt
150ml, ¼pt (²/₃ cup) fromage frais
2 egg whites
2 tsp lemon juice
2 tbsp clear honey
100g, 4 oz seedless grapes

Put the yoghurt and fromage frais into a bowl and mix together. Whisk the egg whites until stiff and fold them into the yoghurt mixture with the lemon juice and honey. Halve the grapes and gently fold into the lemon whip. Chill before serving either in individual glasses or in a glass bowl.

RHUBARB FOOL

900g, 2lb rhubarb, chopped
6 tbsp orange juice
5 tbsp redcurrant jelly
2 tbsp honey
300ml, ½pt (1¼ cups) whipped cream

Put the rhubarb in a saucepan with the orange juice, the redcurrant jelly and the honey. Cover and simmer until soft. Purée or rub through a sieve. When the purée is cold fold in the whipped cream.

GOOSEBERRY FOOL

225g, 8oz gooseberries, topped and tailed
1 tbsp water
2 tbsp honey
25g, 1oz (1 tbsp) sugar
150ml, ¼pt (²/₃ cup) ready-made custard
3 tbsp whipped cream

Put the gooseberries in a saucepan with the honey, sugar and water and cook until soft. Purée or sieve the mixture and fold into the whipped cream and custard.

PEAR AND HONEY PANCAKES

Makes 8 pancakes

Pancake mixture

300ml, ½pt (1¼ cups) milk
100g, 4oz (1 cup) flour
1 egg

Sauce

3 pears, peeled and chopped
2 tbsp honey
1 tsp ground ginger
25g, 1oz (¼ cup) walnuts
4 tbsp water

To make the batter, beat all ingredients together in a food processor, placing first the milk, then the egg, and lastly the flour into the bowl. If you do not have a processor, sift the flour into a bowl, make a well in the centre, add the beaten egg and milk, and gradually draw the flour in and mix well together. Fry small batches of the batter and make up the pancakes. You can make the sauce by beating all the ingredients together in a food processor if you have one. Then heat in a small saucepan and cook for a couple of minutes. Put some sauce in each pancake and roll up. Serve at once.

ORANGE AND
LEMON PANCAKES

Make the pancakes as in the previous recipe.

Filling

225g, 8oz (1 cup) fromage frais
2 tbsp clear honey
rind of 1 lemon
juice of 1 orange

Mix the fromage frais, honey and lemon rind together and spread a spoonful on each pancake. Roll up, dribble a little orange juice on each pancake. Serve straight away.

BAKED FIGS WITH MASCARPONE
AND HAZELNUTS

8 figs, peeled
100g, 4oz (½ cup) mascarpone
50g, 2oz (½ cup) hazelnuts, roasted and chopped
1 tbsp sherry
2 tbsp honey

Halve the figs and lay them in a baking dish. Mix together the mascarpone, sherry, honey and nuts and pour onto the figs. Bake in the oven at gas mark 5, 190°C (375°F) for about 15 minutes.

GRAPEFRUIT AND HONEY
LAYERED PUDDING

This takes a bit of time to prepare but is worth the effort.

50g, 2oz (½ cup) butter
100g, 4oz (1 cup) brown breadcrumbs
25g, 1oz (1tbsp) demerara sugar
14g, ½oz gelatine, or vege-gel (the vegetarian
equivalent)
3 tbsp water
2 grapefruit, peeled and segmented
2 tbsp clear honey
1 egg, separated
150ml, ¼pt (²/₃ cup) plain yoghurt

Heat the butter in a saucepan, add the breadcrumbs and cook, stirring constantly, until crisp. Stir in the sugar and cool on a plate. Soften the gelatine in 3 tablespoons of water. Chop the grapefruit and reserve the juice. Add water to make the grapefruit juice up to 120ml, 4fl oz (½ cup). Add the juice to the gelatine mixture, place over a saucepan of simmering water and stir until dissolved. Remove from the heat and stir in the honey. Beat the egg yolk and yoghurt together, then gradually stir in the honey and gelatine mixture. Cool until almost set. Whisk the egg white and fold into the yoghurt mixture, along with the chopped grapefruit. Place some breadcrumbs in the bottom of a glass dish. Cover with a layer of grapefruit mixture and repeat ending with breadcrumbs. Chill before serving.

POACHED APRICOTS

A very simple but healthy dessert.

450g, 1lb fresh apricots
300ml, ½pt (1¼ cups) water
5 tbsp honey

Put the honey and water into a saucepan and heat gently. Halve the apricots, remove the stones and place in the syrup. Cover and cook slowly. As soon as the apricots are soft take out with a slotted spoon. Boil the syrup to reduce and pour over the apricots.

BAKED HONEY APPLES

4 cooking apples
25g, 1oz (2 tbsp) butter
2 tbsp honey
juice of ½ lemon
4 tbsp hot water

Peel and core the apples. Fill the centres with honey and put a small piece of butter on each. Mix the lemon juice with the water. Put the apples in a baking dish and surround with the lemon water. Bake in the oven at gas mark 4, 180°C (350°F) for 30 minutes until soft, basting them with the liquid every so often. Serve hot with the juice poured over them.

HONEY AND BLACKBERRY
UPSIDE DOWN PUDDING

This is a delicious honey sponge toppped with apples and
blackberries.

100g, 4oz (½ cup) butter
90ml, 3fl oz (¹/₃ cup) honey
100g, 4oz (1 cup) wholemeal flour
1 tsp baking powder
2 eggs, beaten
225g, 8oz blackberries
225g , 8oz eating apples, peeled, cored and chopped
50g, 2oz (¹/₃ cup) granulated sugar

Cream the butter and honey together. Combine the flour and
baking powder and mix into the butter and honey alternately
with the eggs. Grease a 20cm (8in) cake tin. Mix the blackberries, apples and sugar and put in the bottom of the tin. Spoon
the cake mixture on top. Bake in the oven at gas mark 4, 180°C
(350°F) for 30 minutes. Turn the cake out and serve with cream.

HONEYED APPLE AND
LEMON SURPRISE PUDDING

This is yummy and children love the surprises under the light
lemon sponge.

450g, 1lb cooking apples, cored, peeled and sliced
65g, 2½oz (¼ cup + 1 tbsp) butter
2 tbsp honey
100g, 4oz (²/₃ cup) granulated sugar
2 eggs, separated
1 tbsp flour
120ml, 4fl oz (½ cup) milk
rind and juice of 1 lemon

Fry the apple slices in 50g, 2oz (¼ cup) of the butter with the
honey for a few minutes to soften the apples. Place in the base
of a rectangular 20 x 14cm (8 x 5 ½in) pie tin. Mix the remaining butter into the sugar until evenly blended. Add the egg
yolks and mix in the flour. Then add the lemon juice, rind and
milk. Whisk the egg whites and fold into the mixture. Pour
over the apple slices. Half fill a roasting tin with water and
place the pie tin in it. Bake in the oven at gas mark 4, 180°C
(350°F) for 25 minutes.

Tarts and Pastries

Shortcrust Pastry

Honey Tart

Apply Dapply Tart

Walnut and Honey Tart

Hazelnut Tart

Apple and Nut Flan

Glazed Apple and Honey Tart

Baklava

Honey and Poppy Seed Pastries

Sardinian Pastries

SHORTCRUST PASTRY

Many of the following recipes include shortcrust pastry. Here is a standard recipe for pastry which will be enough to line a 20cm (8in) flan dish.

150g, 6oz (1½ cups) plain flour
75g, 3oz (¹/₃ cup) margarine
water

Rub the margarine into the flour with your fingertips until the mixture resembles breadcrumbs. Bind together with a little water until you have a ball of pastry. Roll out on a lightly floured surface.

HONEY TART

This is similar to a treacle tart but is made with honey instead of golden syrup. It is a quick and simple tart to prepare.

1 quantity shortcrust pastry

4 tbsp well-flavoured honey
100g, 4oz (1 cup) brown breadcrumbs

Line a greased 20cm (8in) flan dish with the pastry. Sprinkle the breadcrumbs over the pastry and spoon over the honey. Cook in the oven at gas mark 5, 190°C (375°F) for 20 minutes. Serve hot with cream.

APPLY DAPPLY TART

1 quantity of shortcrust pastry

225g, 8oz (1 cup) mascarpone or full fat cream cheese
½ tsp vanilla essence
2 tbsp honey
juice of ½ lemon
675g, 1½lb eating apples (Cox's Orange Pippins or other
well flavoured crisp apples)
25g, 1oz (2tbsp) butter

Roll out the pastry and line a greased 20cm (8in) flan dish.
Prick and bake blind at gas mark 5, 190°C (375°F) for 15
minutes. Mix together the mascarpone, 1 tablespoon of the
honey, 1 tablespoon of the lemon juice and the vanilla essence.
Fill the pastry case with this mixture and leave in a cool place.
Peel, core and chop up the apples. Fry them in some butter,
add 1 tablespoon of honey and the remaining lemon juice.
Fry the apples rapidly until the juice has evaporated. Pile the
apples over the mascarpone and serve straight away.

WALNUT AND HONEY TART

1 quantity shortcrust pastry

4 tbsp clear honey
75g, 3oz (¾ cup) brown breadcrumbs
2 tbsp dark brown sugar
juice of ½ orange
3 eggs
100g, 4oz (1 cup) chopped walnuts

Line a greased 20cm (8in) flan dish with the pastry. Prick and bake blind at gas mark 5, 190°C (375°F) for 15 minutes. Mix the honey, breadcrumbs and sugar, gradually beating in the eggs and the orange juice. Spoon the walnuts over the pastry case and pour over the filling. Return to the oven and bake for 20 minutes or until the filling is set.

HAZELNUT TART

1 quantity shortcrust pastry

225g, 8oz (2 cups) hazelnuts
50g, 2oz (½ cup) light brown sugar
50g, 2oz (¼ cup) butter
2 large eggs
150g, 6oz (½ cup) honey
Juice of ½ lemon
2 egg whites

Line a greased 20cm (8in) flan dish with the pastry. Finely chop the hazelnuts (this can be done most effectively in a processor). Beat the butter and sugar together and gradually add the beaten eggs. Add honey and lemon juice and beat. Whisk the egg whites and add the hazelnuts. Fold into the honey mixture and pour into the pastry case. Bake at gas mark 5, 180°C (350°F) for about 30 minutes.

APPLE AND NUT FLAN

1 quantity shortcrust pastry

450g, 1lb cooking apples, peeled, cored and sliced
50g, 2oz (¼ cup) butter
3 tbsp honey
50g, 2oz (½ cup) chopped nuts
½ tsp cinnamon
sprinkling of nutmeg

Line a greased 20cm (8in) flan dish with the pastry. Slice the apples and layer them inside the pastry case. Heat the butter, honey and cinnamon together and pour over the apples. Sprinkle the chopped nuts and nutmeg over the top. Bake in the oven at gas mark 4, 180°C (350°F) for 25 minutes.

GLAZED APPLE
AND HONEY TART

75g, 3oz (¹/₃ cup) butter
75g , 3oz (¾ cup) wholewheat flour
75g , 3oz (¾ cup) plain flour
3 egg yolks
3 tbsp water
300ml, ½pt (1¼ cups) apple purée
4 tbsp honey
2 tbsp ground almonds
2 Cox's Orange Pippins or other eating apples, thinly sliced

Rub the butter into the flours. Beat one of the egg yolks and 2 tablespoons of water into the flour and knead to form a soft dough. Roll out and line a greased 22.5cm (9in) flan dish. Mix the apple purée with 2 tablespoons of honey, the remaining egg yolks and the almonds. Spread over the pastry base. Arrange the apple slices on top and bake in the oven at gas mark 4, 180°C (350°F) for about 30 minutes. Warm the remaining honey and brush over the apples before serving.

BAKLAVA

Baklava is probably the most famous Greek dessert and is eaten all over the Middle East. It is sticky and gorgeous.

Pastry

325g, 12oz (3 cups) walnuts
75g, 3oz (½ cup) sugar
½ tsp cinnamon
2 tbsp honey
450g, 1lb filo pastry
125g, 5oz (⅔ cup) butter, melted

Syrup

300g, 11oz (1⅔ cups) sugar
300ml, ½pt (1¼ cups) water
1 tbsp lemon juice

Cut the sheets of filo pastry to fit into a medium sized roasting tin. Mix together the walnuts, cinnamon, sugar and honey. Put half the sheets of filo pastry in the tin, brushing each carefully with melted butter. Spread half the nutty mixture over the pastry, then top with a couple more sheets of pastry and with the rest of the nutty mixture. Cover with remaining sheets of filo pastry, brushing with butter. Cut the pastry into diamond shapes and bake in the oven at gas mark 4, 180°C (350°F) for 20 minutes. Increase the oven temperature to gas mark 5, 190°C (375°F) and cook for a further 15 minutes. Meanwhile make the syrup by putting the water, sugar and lemon juice together in a saucepan and heating gently until the sugar has dissolved. Bring to the boil and boil for 10 minutes. Take the pastry out of the oven and pour over the syrup. Leave to be absorbed and become moist, before cutting up and serving.

HONEY AND
POPPY SEED PASTRIES

Makes 12 pastries

225g, 8oz puff pastry
75g, 3oz (¾ cup) almonds
75g, 3oz (¾ cup) walnuts
50g, 2oz (½ cup) sesame seeds
2 tbsp poppy seeds
2 tbsp clear honey
1 egg white, beaten
icing sugar

Roll out the pastry and cut into about 12 squares. Grind the almonds, walnuts and sesame seeds together or put them in a food processor. Stir in the poppy seeds and mix in the honey. Place a spoonful of the mixture in the centre of each pastry square. Cover the filling by folding the four corners over it and pressing down in the centre. Moistening the edges may help. Brush with the beaten egg white and place on greased baking sheets. Cook in the oven at gas mark 4, 180°C (350°F) for 20 minutes. Cool, dust with icing sugar and serve.

SARDINIAN PASTRIES

This is a traditional recipe in Sardinia where they use honey
as a sweetener rather than sugar.

Pastry

450g, 1lb (4 cups) strong flour
4 eggs
50g, 2oz (¼ cup) butter

Filling

450g, 1lb mozzarella cheese, cubed
450g, 1lb (2 cups) ricotta
grated rind of 1 orange

225g, 8oz (¾ cup) warmed honey

Make the pastry by mixing the flour with the eggs and kneading a little before adding the butter, a little at a time. Knead to
an elastic dough, adding a little water if you need to.Roll out
the pastry and cut into small circles, about 5cm (2in) in diam-
eter. For the filling, mix together the cheeses and orange rind.
Put two teaspoons in the centre of the pastry rounds and cover
with lids. Seal the edges using a finger, moistened with water.
Deep fry the pastries in oil - they will only need a few minutes.
Serve straight away with honey poured over them.

Steamed Puddings

Steamed Honey Pudding

Cranberry and Honey Steamed Pudding

Steamed Lemon and Honey Pudding

Irish Steamed Oat and Honey Pudding

STEAMED HONEY PUDDING

This is a simple steamed pudding and a good one to start
with if you haven't made this sort of pudding before.

2 eggs
100g, 4oz (²/₃ cup) caster sugar
100g, 4oz (½ cup) margarine
100g, 4oz (1cup) self-raising flour
2 tbsp honey

Mix the first four ingredients together in the usual way for a
cake sponge. Pour the honey into the bottom of a greased
600ml (1pt) pudding basin and put the cake mixture on top.
Cover with a piece of greaseproof paper folded with a pleat
to allow space for the pudding to rise. Secure with string or a
rubber band round the pudding basin. Place the pudding in a
steamer or a large saucepan and fill with boiling water to come
half way up the sides of the basin. Cover and simmer for 2½
hours. Serve with some warmed honey.

CRANBERRY AND HONEY STEAMED PUDDING

150g, 6oz (1½ cups) self-raising flour
1 tsp baking powder
1 tsp cinnamon
½ tsp ground cloves
75g, 3oz (¾ cup) breadcrumbs
100g, 4oz shredded suet
150g, 6oz fresh cranberries
180ml, 6fl oz (¾ cup) milk
1 egg
4 tbsp warmed honey

Sift the flour, baking powder and spices in a bowl. Stir in the breadcrumbs, suet and cranberries. Whisk the egg with the milk and stir in the honey. Grease a 600ml (1pt) pudding basin and pour the mixture in. Cover with a piece of greaseproof paper folded with a pleat to allow space for the pudding to rise. Secure with string or a rubber band round the pudding basin. Place the pudding in a steamer or a large saucepan and fill with boiling water to come half way up the sides of the basin. Cover and simmer for 2½ hours.

STEAMED LEMON AND
HONEY PUDDING

2 tbsp honey
50g, 2oz (½ cup) self-raising flour
1 tsp baking powder
100g, 4oz (1 cup) breadcrumbs
150g, 6oz suet
100g, 4oz (²/₃ cup) caster sugar
3 eggs
3 tbsp lemon curd
grated rind and juice of 1 lemon

Spoon the honey into the bottom of a greased 600ml (1pt) pudding basin. Sift the flour and baking powder into a bowl. Add the breadcrumbs, suet and sugar and stir together. In a small bowl beat the eggs and the lemon curd together and stir into the pudding mixture. Finally stir in the lemon juice and rind. Pour into the pudding basin. Cover with a piece of greaseproof paper folded with a pleat to allow space for the pudding to rise. Secure with string or a rubber band round the pudding basin. Place the pudding in a steamer or a large saucepan and fill with boiling water to come half way up the sides of the basin. Cover and simmer for 2½ hours.

IRISH STEAMED OAT AND
HONEY PUDDING

450ml, ¾pt (1¾ cups) milk
150g, 6oz (2¹/₃ cups) porridge oats
50g, 2oz (¹/₃ cup) caster sugar
2 tbsp clear honey
25g, 1oz (2 tbsp) butter
grated rind of 1 orange
½ tsp cinnamon
3 eggs, separated

Bring the milk to the boil in a saucepan, add the oats and cook gently for a few minutes. Beat in the sugar, honey, butter, orange rind and cinnamon and mix well. Remove from the heat and beat in the egg yolks. Whisk the egg whites and fold into the mixture. Turn into a greased 1.2 litre (2pt) pudding basin. Cover with a piece of greaseproof paper folded with a pleat to allow space for the pudding to rise. Secure with string or a rubber band round the pudding basin. Place the pudding in a steamer or a large saucepan and fill with boiling water to come half way up the sides of the basin. Cover and simmer for 2 hours. Turn out and dribble extra honey over the pudding.

Cheesecakes

Honey Cheesecake

Honey and Walnut Cheesecake

Blueberry Cheesecake

HONEY CHEESECAKE

100g, 4oz (1cup) plain flour
25g, 1oz (¼ cup) fine semolina
75g, 3oz (¹/₃ cup) butter
1 tbsp caster sugar
water to mix

Filling

325g, 12oz (1½ cups) cream cheese
3 eggs, separated
3 tbsp honey
3 tbsp sultanas
1 tbsp mixed peel
1 tbsp semolina
3 tbsp cream
1 tbsp lemon juice
1 tbsp sugar
1 tsp cinnamon

To make the pastry sift together the flour and semolina and rub in the butter. Stir in the sugar. Mix to a stiff dough with a little water. Roll out the pastry and line a deep greased 20cm (8in) flan tin with it. To make the filling, sprinkle sultanas and mixed peel over the bottom of the pastry case. Mix up the cream cheese, egg yolks, honey, semolina, cream and lemon juice - this can be done in a food processor. Lastly, whisk the egg whites and fold them in. Pour over the fruit and sprinkle with cinnamon and the tablespoon of sugar. Bake in the oven at gas mark 4, 180°C (350°F) for about 35 minutes.

HONEY AND WALNUT
CHEESECAKE

Base
150g, 6oz digestive biscuits, crushed
75g, 3oz (¹/₃ cup) melted butter

Filling
225g, 8oz (1 cup) cream cheese
3 eggs, separated
4 tbsp set honey
25g, 1oz (¼ cup) plain flour
4 tbsp whipped cream
100g, 4oz (1 cup) walnuts, chopped
50g, 2oz (¹/₃ cup) caster sugar

Topping
2 tbsp honey

Mix the crushed digestive biscuits into the melted butter and use to line a 22.5cm (9in) flan dish. Beat the cream cheese and beat in the egg yolks, honey, flour, cream and chopped walnuts. Whisk the egg whites in a separate bowl and whisk in the sugar. Fold this mixture into the cream cheese. Place on the biscuit base and smooth the surface. Cook in the oven at gas mark 3, 160°C (325°F) for about an hour and then leave the cheesecake to cool. Melt the remaining honey for the topping and pour over the cheesecake. Chill and serve.

BLUEBERRY CHEESECAKE

Base
150g, 6oz digestive biscuits
75g, 3oz (¹/₃ cup) butter

Filling
225g, 8oz (1 cup) cream cheese
1 small carton soured cream
4 tbsp lemon juice
75g, 3oz (½ cup) caster sugar
grated rind and juice of 1 small orange
2 tsp gelatine or vege-gel (the vegetarian equivalent)

Topping
325g, 12oz blueberries
2 tbsp lemon juice
2 tbsp honey
2 tsp cornflour

Crush the biscuits, mix with the melted butter and use to line a 20cm (8in) deep flan tin. Chill. Beat the cream cheese and soured cream together and add the lemon juice, sugar and orange rind. Dissolve the gelatine in the orange juice over a pan of simmering water. Stir into the cheese mixture. Pour over the biscuit base. For the topping, cook the blueberries with the lemon juice and sweeten with the honey. Mix the cornflour with a little water and add to the blueberries. Bring back to the boil and cook until thickened. Cool and chill. Just before serving, spread the blueberry mixture on top of the cheesecake.

Ice-Creams

Easy Honey Ice-Cream

Brown Bread Ice-Cream

Honey and Hazelnut Ice-Cream

Mascarpone and Honey Ice-Cream

Orange and Honey Ice-Cream

Honey and Banana Ice-Cream

Poppy Seed Ice-Cream

Mint Ice-Cream

Plum Ice-Cream

Passionfruit Ice-Cream

Gin and Lavender Flavoured Ice-Cream

Cinnamon Ice-Cream

Coffee and Almond Ice-Cream

Butterscotch Ice-Cream

Watermelon and Raspberry Cream Ice

Redcurrant and Honey Ice-Cream

Peach and Hazelnut Ice-Cream

EASY HONEY ICE-CREAM

225g, 8oz (¾ cup) clear aromatic honey
4 egg yolks
450ml, ¾pt (1¾ cups) whipped cream
lemon juice to taste

Heat the honey in a saucepan with 4 tablespoons of water to just below boiling point. Whisk the egg yolks in a bowl until thick and creamy and then whisk in the hot honey. Return the mixture to the pan and cook gently, whisking until the mixture thickens. Remove from the heat and continue whisking until the mixture is cold. Fold the cream into the honey mixture and add lemon juice to taste. Pour into a freezer container and freeze until firm.

BROWN BREAD ICE-CREAM

75g, 3oz (¾ cup) brown breadcrumbs
75g, 3oz (½ cup) demerara sugar
2 eggs, separated
1 tbsp honey
450ml, ¾pt (1¾ cups) whipped cream

Mix the breadcrumbs and sugar together. Place on a baking sheet and bake in the oven at gas mark 4, 180°C (350°F) until the sugar has melted and the breadcrumbs have caramelised. Cool the mixture. Beat the egg yolks and honey together. Whisk the egg whites and fold into the whipped cream. Then carefully fold this in to the egg yolk mixture. Stir in the breadcrumbs and sugar, put into a freezer container and freeze until firm.

115

HONEY AND HAZELNUT
ICE-CREAM

50g, 2oz (¼ cup) butter
100g, 4 oz ('/₃ cup) set honey
450ml, ¾pt (1¾ cups) milk
100g, 4oz (1 cup) hazelnuts, ground
50g, 2oz (½ cup) demerara sugar
3 egg yolks
1 tbsp gelatine or vege-gel (the vegetarian equivalent)
300ml, ½pt (1¼ cups) whipped cream
3 tbsp brandy

Melt the butter and honey with the milk in a saucepan. Bring to
the boil, add the nuts, cover and leave to cool for 10 minutes.
Beat the egg yolks with the sugar in a bowl. Gradually stir in
the flavoured milk. Return to a saucepan and cook gently stirring
constantly until the mixture thickens. Do not allow to boil.
Dissolve the gelatine in 3 tablespoons of water in a small bowl.
Stir the gelatine into the custard. Leave until cool and fold in
the cream and brandy. Pour into a freezer container and freeze
until firm.

MASCARPONE AND
HONEY ICE-CREAM

This ice-cream goes well with a fruity dessert. It goes particularly well with the Blackcurrant Kissel.

225g, 8oz (1 cup) mascarpone
2 tbsp honey
2 eggs, separated
2 tbsp brandy

Whisk the egg yolks and whisk in the honey and the brandy. Whisk in the mascarpone and lastly whisk the egg whites until stiff and fold in to the mascarpone mixture. Transfer into a freezer container and freeze until firm.

ORANGE AND HONEY ICE-CREAM

2 oranges
2 egg yolks
4 tbsp clear honey
300ml, ½pt (1¼ cups) Greek yoghurt
150ml, ¼ pt (²/₃ cup) whipped cream

Grate the rind of the oranges and mix with the egg yolks and honey. Squeeze the oranges and add the juice to the egg yolk mixture. Pour into a saucepan and heat gently, stirring until thickened. Leave to cool. Fold the orange mixture into the yoghurt then whisk into the cream. Pour into a freezer container and freeze until firm.

HONEY AND
BANANA ICE-CREAM

Bananas and honey go really well together and this ice-cream is very popular with children.

450g, 1lb bananas
150ml, ¼pt (²/₃ cup) double cream
150ml, ¼pt (²/₃ cup) plain yoghurt
2 tbsp lemon juice
2 tbsp set honey
2 egg whites

Mash the bananas in a bowl. Blend in the cream, yoghurt, lemon juice and honey until smooth. Pour into a container, cover and freeze, beating twice at 45 minute intervals. Whisk the egg whites and fold into the banana mixture after the second beating.

POPPY SEED ICE-CREAM

4 eggs, separated
100g, 4oz (²/₃ cup) caster sugar
1 tbsp clear honey
240ml, 8fl oz (1 cup) milk
1 tsp vanilla essence
450ml, ¾pt (1¾ cups) whipped cream
50g, 2oz (¼ cup) poppy seeds

Whisk the egg yolks, sugar and honey together in a bowl over a pan of simmering water until the mixture becomes thick. Bring the milk and vanilla essence to the boil and pour slowly onto the egg yolk mixture, while continuing to whisk. Fold this mixture into the whipped cream and lastly mix in the poppy seeds. Pour into a freezer container and freeze until firm.

MINT ICE-CREAM

This is one of my favourite ice-creams. The mint gives it a lovely flavour.

4 tbsp clear honey
150ml, ¼ pt (²/₃ cup) water
2 tbsp chopped mint
1 tbsp lemon juice
150g, 6oz (¾ cup) cream cheese
150ml, ¼pt (²/₃ cup) soured cream

Melt the honey in a saucepan with water. Then boil this syrup for 5 minutes. Stir in the lemon juice and chopped mint and leave for about 30 minutes so that the syrup absorbs the flavour of mint. Beat the cream and cheese together in a bowl and strain the syrup into the cream mixture. Transfer to a freezer container and freeze until firm, beating twice at hourly intervals.

PLUM ICE-CREAM

450g, 1lb plums, halved and stoned
2 tbsp clear honey
75g, 3oz (½ cup) demerara sugar
rind and juice of 1 lemon
225g, 8oz (1 cup) mascarpone
300ml, ½pt (1¼ cups) double cream
2 egg whites

Cook the plums with the honey, sugar and lemon rind and juice until they are soft. Purée the plums. Beat the mascarpone and cream together and gradually beat in the plum purée. When the mixture is cool enough, transfer to a freezer container and freeze until just becoming firm. Whisk the egg whites and fold them into the half frozen plum mixture. Return to the freezer and freeze until firm.

PASSIONFRUIT ICE-CREAM

5 passionfruit
4 egg yolks
125g, 5oz (¾ cup) caster sugar
240ml, 8fl oz (1 cup) milk
1 tbsp clear honey
225g, 8oz (1 cup) mascarpone

Whisk together the egg yolks and sugar. Heat the milk until it is on the point of boiling and then whisk into the egg yolk mixture. Return to the heat and cook, stirring all the time until the custard thickens. Remove from the heat and continue to stir as the mixture cools. Add the spoonful of honey and the mascarpone. Stir until smooth. Cut up the passionfruit, discard skins and purée flesh in a food processor. Then sieve the passionfruit pulp to separate it from the seeds. Mix the fruit purée into the mascarpone mixture and transfer to a freezer container. Freeze and whisk twice at hourly intervals.

GIN AND LAVENDER
FLAVOURED ICE-CREAM

Strictly for adults only! This ice-cream has a lovely creamy
texture.

6 tbsp gin
1 tbsp lavender flowers
6 egg yolks
175g, 7oz ($^2/_3$ cup) clear honey
300ml, ½pt (1¼ cups) double cream

Warm the gin a little and pour over the lavender. Leave to
absorb the lavender flavour for an hour. Strain the gin through
a fine sieve extracting as much from the flowers as possible. In
a large bowl beat the egg yolks. Gently heat the honey and
then pour over the egg yolks while continuing to whisk. Cool
this mixture before adding the flavoured gin. Whip the cream
and fold it in. Transfer to a freezer container and freeze until
firm.

CINNAMON ICE-CREAM

150ml, ¼pt (²/₃ cup) milk
2 cinnamon sticks
4 eggs, separated
25g, 1oz (1 tbsp) icing sugar
2 tsp ground cinnamon
100g, 4oz ((¹/₃ cup) clear honey
150ml, ¼pt (²/₃ cup) soured cream
125g, 5oz (²/₃ cup) cream cheese

Heat the milk with the cinnamon sticks to just below boiling point. Cover and leave to absorb the flavour of the cinnamon. Beat the egg yolks, sift in the icing sugar and ground cinnamon and beat well together. Remove the cinnamon sticks from the milk and stir in the honey. Heat until just below boiling point again. Pour on to the egg yolks and whisk together. Beat the soured cream and cream cheese together and whisk into the egg yolk mixture. Finally, whisk the egg whites and fold them in very carefully. Transfer to a freezer container and freeze until firm.

COFFEE AND ALMOND
ICE-CREAM

300ml, ½pt (1¼ cups) Greek yoghurt
2 tbsp coffee essence
2 tbsp set honey
50g, 2oz (½ cup) ground almonds
2 egg whites

Beat together the yoghurt, honey and coffee essence. Stir in the ground almonds. Whisk the egg whites and fold into the coffee mixture. Pour into a freezer container and freeze.

BUTTERSCOTCH ICE-CREAM

3 tbsp honey
75g, 3oz (¾ cup) brown sugar
50g, 2oz (¼ cup) butter
1 tsp lemon juice
300ml, ½pt (1¼ cups) Greek yoghurt
150ml, ¼pt (²/₃ cup) double cream

Melt together the honey, brown sugar and butter. Cool, add the lemon juice and stir this mixture into the yoghurt. Whip the double cream and fold into the butterscotch mixture. Pour into a freezer container and freeze until firm.

WATERMELON AND RASPBERRY CREAM ICE

4 tbsp clear honey
juice of ½ lemon
225g, 8oz raspberries
1 watermelon
150ml, ¼pt (²/₃ cup) Greek yoghurt
150ml, ¼pt (²/₃ cup) whipping cream
caster sugar to taste

Whisk the honey and lemon juice. Whip the cream. Fold the honey and lemon into the cream and yoghurt. Fold in the raspberries. Cut the watermelon in half. Remove the seeds and purée the flesh. Add this to the cream mixture. Have a taste and add some caster sugar if it is still not sweet enough. Pour into a freezer container and freeze until firm.

REDCURRANT AND
HONEY ICE-CREAM

My children love this ice-cream.

450g, 1lb redcurrants
3 tbsp clear honey
3 egg yolks
75g, 3oz (½ cup) granulated sugar
120ml, 4fl oz (½ cup) water
300ml, ½pt (1¼ cups) whipping cream

Purée the redcurrants and sieve them to remove all the seeds. Mix the honey into the redcurrant purée. Meanwhile dissolve the sugar in the water and boil for five minutes. Beat the egg yolks together until thick. Pour the sugar syrup onto the egg yolks while continuing to whisk until you have a frothy, creamy mixture. Whip the cream and fold into the egg mixture along with the redcurrant purée. When everything is evenly blended pop into a freezer container and freeze for an hour. Take out and beat the mixture to help reduce ice crystals and beat again after another hour. Return to the freezer and freeze until firm.

PEACH AND HAZELNUT
ICE-CREAM

4 large peaches or 6 small peaches
4 tbsp honey
3 egg yolks
150ml, ¼pt (²/₃ cup) whipped cream
50g, 2oz (½ cup) chopped hazelnuts
few drops of lemon juice

Peel the peaches, remove the stones and purée the flesh. Put the honey and one tablespoon of water in a saucepan and heat gently to melt the honey. Then bring to boiling point. Whisk the egg yolks and pour the hot syrup in a steady stream on to the egg yolks whisking all the time. Over a pan of simmering water, continue to whisk until the mixture thickens. Whisk the peach purée and hazelnuts into the egg yolk mixture. Fold in the cream and add a little lemon juice. Pour into a freezer container and freeze until firm.

TEA-TIME TREATS

Granary Bread

Granary Loaf

Honey Bread

Apple and Walnut Tea-Bread

Banana Bread

Malt Loaf

Lardy Cake

Honey Buns

Apple and Honey Scones

Bran Muffins

Yoghurt and Honey Squares

Parkin

Lemon-Flavoured Honey Cake

Rich Honey Cake

Buttery Honey Cake

Somerset Apple Cake

Spicy Carrot Cake

Nutty Carrot Cake

Marmalade Cake

Elizabethan Parsnip Cake

Walnut Cake

Spicy Honey Ring

Coffee and Honey Cake

Chocolate Cake

Honey Swiss Roll

Hazelnut Swiss Roll

Honey and Lemon Cakes
Brandy Snaps
Honey Flapjacks
Banana Flapjacks
Honey and Apple Flapjacks
Banana and Chocolate Crunch
Muesli Fudge Slices
Pecan Fudge Bars
Chocolate and Honey Muesli Slice
Toffee Chocolate Crunch
Chocolate and Honey Biscuit Cake
Sunflower and Honey Crunches
Sesame Seed Slices
Peanut Shortbread
Peanut Butter Cookies
Peanut and Honey Squares
Gingerbread Men
Shortbread and Honey Bars
Honeyed Oatmeal Biscuits
Rice Krispie Crunchies
Honey and Mincemeat Fingers
Cinnamon Biscuits
Honey Cookies
Honey Nut Cookies
Walnut Cookies
Muesli Cookies

GRANARY BREAD

Makes 3 loaves

This bread has a nice granary taste but has the lightness
of a brioche because of the extra butter. The good thing
is you don't have to do any kneading.

1 tbsp honey
700ml 1¼pt (3 cups) warm milk
3 sachets easy-blend dried yeast
1.35kg, 3lb (12 cups) granary flour
3 eggs
1 tsp salt
150g, 6oz (¾ cup) melted butter

Dissolve the honey in 150ml, ¼pt of milk. Mix the yeast
into the flour and add the eggs, salt and melted butter. Add
the milk and honey mixture with the rest of the milk and
mix to a dough. The dough will be quite wet so beat with a
spoon. Cover the bowl with a damp tea-towel and leave to
rise in a warm place for an hour. Knock back the dough
and shape into three loaves. Place into three greased 1kg
(2lb) loaf tins and leave to rise for another 30 minutes.
Cook in a pre-heated oven at gas mark 6, 200°C (425°F)
for about 40 minutes or until the loaves sound hollow when
tapped.

GRANARY LOAF

Makes 3 loaves

If you want to make a healthier granary loaf, without so much butter, then try this alternative recipe.

1.35kg, 3lb (2cups) granary flour
900ml, 1½ pt (3¾ cups) hot water
3 sachets easy-blend dried yeast
1 tsp salt
2 tbsp honey

Dissolve the salt and honey in the water. Mix the yeast with the flour and stir in the water and honey mixture. Gather into a ball and knead for 5 minutes before cutting into three. Pack into well greased 1kg (2lb) loaf tins, cover with a damp tea towel and leave to rise for 30 minutes. Bake in a pre-heated oven at gas mark 7, 220°C (450°F) for 40 minutes.

HONEY BREAD

Makes 1 large loaf

40g, 1½oz (½ cup) oats
300ml, ½pt (1¼ cups) milk
30ml, 1fl oz (2 tbsp) sunflower oil
1 tbsp brown sugar
1 tbsp clear honey
150g, 6oz (1½ cups) strong white flour
225g, 8oz (2 cups) wholemeal flour
75g, 3oz (1 cup) soya flour
25g, 1oz (½ cup) bran
1 tsp salt
1 sachet easy-blend dried yeast
1 egg, beaten

Heat the milk until just below boiling point and pour over the oats. Add the oil, sugar and honey and stir well. Leave to cool until hand-hot. Mix the flours, bran, salt and yeast in a large bowl. Pour in the oat mixture and egg and mix to a dough. Knead on a floured surface for at least five minutes until smooth. Shape into a loaf. Turn into a greased 1kg (2lb) loaf tin. Cover with a damp tea-towel and leave to rise for 30 mintues in a warm place. Bake in the oven at gas mark 6, 200°C (400°F) for about 30 minutes.

APPLE AND WALNUT TEA-BREAD

Makes 2 loaves

1 large cooking apple, peeled, cored and chopped
50g, 2oz (½ cup) walnuts, chopped
100g, 4oz (1 cup) soft brown sugar
100g, 4oz (½ cup) margarine
100g, 4oz (²/₃ cup) raisins
2 eggs
1 tbsp honey
150g, 6oz (1½ cups) self-raising flour
50g, 2oz (½ cup) wholemeal flour
1 tsp mixed spice

Place all the ingredients in a large bowl and beat well until everything is well-blended. Put the mixture into two greased 1kg (2lb) loaf tins and bake in the oven at gas mark 4, 180°C (350°F) for 1¼ hours. When cooked, turn out onto a wire rack and serve sliced with butter.

BANANA BREAD

Makes 1 loaf

225g, 8oz (2 cups) self-raising flour
½ tsp mixed spice
125g, 5oz (¾ cup) caster sugar
450g, 1lb bananas, ripe
1 tbsp honey
50g, 2oz (½ cup) walnuts (optional)
2 eggs, beaten

Sift the flour and mixed spice together and stir in the sugar. Mash the bananas and beat into the flour mixture with the eggs, honey and walnuts. Spoon the mixture into a greased 1kg (2lb) loaf tin and bake in the oven at gas mark 4, 180°C (350°F) for about 1 hour.

MALT LOAF

Makes 2 small loaves

450g, 1lb (4 cups) plain flour
1 sachet easy-blend dried yeast
100g, 4oz (²/₃ cup) raisins or sultanas
50g, 2oz (½ cup) caster sugar
4 tbsp malt extract
1 tbsp black treacle
50g, 2oz (¼ cup) butter
1 tbsp sugar

Glaze
2 tbsp honey
1 tbsp water

Stir the yeast and raisins or sultanas into the flour. Form a well in the centre. Gently heat the sugar, malt extract, treacle and butter with 180ml, 6fl oz (¾ cup) of water until the butter has melted and the sugar dissolved. Allow to cool a little, then pour into the well in the flour. Draw in the dry ingredients and mix to a dough. Knead until firm. Divide in half and shape into 2 loaves. Grease 2 450g (1lb) loaf tins and leave the dough to rise in the tins for 1 hour, covered with a damp tea-towel. Then put the loaves in a preheated oven at gas mark 6, 200°C (400°F) for about 25 minutes. Turn out on a wire rack. Dissolve the honey with a little water to make the glaze and brush over the top of each loaf.

LARDY CAKE

Makes 2 cakes

450g, 1lb (4 cups) strong white flour
1 tsp salt
1 sachet easy-blend dried yeast
2 tsp caster sugar
1 egg, beaten
240ml, 8fl oz (1 cup) milk

Filling

100g, 4oz (²/₃ cup) currants
4 tbsp honey
100g, 4oz (½ cup) lard

Stir the yeast, flour, salt and sugar together. Warm the milk and add to the flour with the egg. Mix to a firm dough and knead until smooth and elastic. Cover with a damp tea-towel and leave in a warm place to rise. Roll out the dough into a rectangle. Mix the three filling ingredients and spread some over the dough. Fold into three layers and roll out again. Spread on the rest of the filling, refold and roll out another couple of times. Shape to fit 2 greased 20cm (8in) cake tins. Leave to rise again. Then bake in the oven at gas mark 7, 220°C (450°F) for about 30 minutes.

HONEY BUNS

Makes 14 buns

75g, 3oz (¼ cup) honey
50g, 2oz (⅓ cup) granulated sugar
50g, 2oz (¼ cup) margarine
100g, 4oz (1 cup) plain flour
½ tsp bicarbonate of soda
25g, 1oz (¼ cup) chopped walnuts
25g, 1oz (¼ cup) ground almonds
1 egg, beaten
100g, 4oz (¾ cup) sifted icing sugar

Put the honey, sugar and margarine into a saucepan and cook over a low heat - do not allow to boil. Sift together the flour and bicarbonate of soda and stir them into the melted mixture with the chopped walnuts, almonds and egg. Mix together well and divide between greased bun or patty tins, filling each just over half full. Bake at gas mark 4, 180°C (350°F) for about 15 minutes. Then transfer to a wire tray and cool. To ice, mix the icing sugar with a little water and spread over the top of each bun.

APPLE AND HONEY SCONES

Makes 8 - 10 scones

100g, 4oz (1 cup) self-raising flour
75g, 3oz (¾ cup) self-raising wholemeal flour
large pinch of salt
½ tsp cinnamon
50g, 2oz (¼ cup) butter or margarine
2 eating apples, peeled, cored and grated
4 tbsp honey
5 tbsp milk

Sift the flours with the salt and cinnamon. Add the butter or margarine and rub with your fingertips until the mixture resembles breadcrumbs. Add the grated apples, honey and milk and bind the mixture into a dough. Place the dough on a lightly floured surface and knead until smooth. Roll it out until 1.5cm (¾in) thick. Cut into circles or triangles and place on a warmed baking sheet in a pre-heated oven at gas mark 7, 220°C (450°F). Bake for 10 minutes or until well risen and golden. Serve warm with butter and jam or honey.

BRAN MUFFINS

Makes 6 - 8 muffins

125g, 5oz (1¼ cups) wholemeal flour
2 tsp baking powder
2 eggs, beaten
240ml, 8fl oz (1 cup) yoghurt
pinch of salt
75g, 3oz (2 cups) bran
2 tbsp honey
2 tbsp sunflower oil
2 tbsp soya flour

Sieve the wholemeal flour with the baking powder and add the beaten eggs. Mix in the yoghurt and gradually incorporate all the other ingredients. Mix all together well. The mixture will be quite runny. Fill greased muffin cases or bun tins with the mixture and bake in the oven at gas mark 6, 200°C (400°F) for about 20 minutes.

YOGHURT AND HONEY SQUARES

Base

125g, 5oz digestive or other biscuits
1 tbsp honey
65g, 2½oz (¼ cup) butter

Filling

1 small carton yoghurt
225g, 8oz (1 cup) cream cheese
2 tbsp honey
1 tsp grated lemon rind
½ tsp vanilla essence
2 tsp gelatine or vege-gel (the vegetarian equivalent)
1 tbsp water

To make the base, crush the biscuits and melt the butter and honey. Mix all well together and use to line a greased square 20cm (8in) tin. For the filling, beat together the yoghurt, cream cheese, honey, vanilla and lemon rind. Fold in the gelatine which has been softened in the water. Pour onto the base and leave to set firm before cutting into squares.

PARKIN

100g, 4oz (½ cup) butter or margarine
100g, 4oz (¹/₃ cup) honey
100g, 4oz (1 cup) dark brown sugar
100g, 4oz (1 cup) self-raising flour
100g, 4oz (¾ cup) medium oatmeal
1 tsp ground ginger
1 tsp cinnamon
1 large egg, beaten
6 tbsp milk

Melt the butter or margarine, honey and sugar together over a low heat. Sift the flour, ginger and cinnamon into a bowl, stir in the oatmeal and add the melted mixture with the beaten egg and the milk. Pour the mixture into a greased 27.5 x 17.5cm (11 x 7in) baking tin and bake in the oven at gas mark 3, 160°C (325°F) for about an hour.

LEMON-FLAVOURED HONEY CAKE

This is a reasonably healthy cake since it has no fat.

3 eggs, separated
2 tbsp caster sugar
3 tbsp honey
grated rind of 1 lemon
50g, 2oz (½ cup) cornflour
65g, 2½oz (½ cup)self-raising flour

Whisk the egg yolks with the sugar, honey, and lemon rind until thick and creamy. Sift in the cornflour and mix. Fold in stiffly whipped egg whites with the flour. Line a 20cm (8in) cake tin with greaseproof paper. Turn the mixture into the tin and bake in the oven at gas mark 4, 180°C (350°F) for 25 minutes. Turn out and dust with icing sugar.

RICH HONEY CAKE

150g, 6oz (¾ cup) margarine or butter
150g, 6oz (½ cup) honey
3 eggs, beaten
225g, 8oz (2 cups) self-raising flour

Filling

150g, 6oz (1 cup) icing sugar
75g, 3oz (¹/₃ cup) butter

To make the sponge, cream together the margarine or butter and honey. Gradually add the beaten eggs alternately with the flour. When all is mixed together well spoon into a greased 20cm (8in) cake tin and bake in the oven at gas mark 5, 190°C (375°F) for 30 minutes. When cooked, cool and split in half. Make the filling by mixing together the butter and icing sugar and use to sandwich the cake together.

BUTTERY HONEY CAKE

125g, 5oz ($^2/_3$ cup) butter
100g, 4oz (1 cup) light brown sugar
150g, 6oz (½ cup) clear honey
1 tbsp milk
200g, 7oz (1¾ cups) self-raising flour
2 eggs

Put the butter, sugar, honey and milk in a saucepan and place over a low heat until the butter has melted and the sugar has dissolved. Cool slightly and then beat the eggs into the mixture alternately with spoonfuls of flour. Pour into a greased 27.5 x 17.5cm (11 x 7in) rectangular tin and bake in the oven at gas mark 4, 180°C (350°F) for 30 minutes. Turn out onto a wire rack, leave to cool and cut into pieces.

SOMERSET APPLE CAKE

100g, 4oz (½ cup) butter
150g, 6oz (1½ cups) dark brown sugar
2 eggs, beaten
225g, 8oz (2 cups) plain wholemeal flour
1 tsp ground mixed spice
1 tsp ground cinnamon
2 tsp baking powder
450g, 1lb cooking apples, peeled, cored and sliced
3-4 tbsp milk
1 tbsp clear honey
1 tbsp demerara sugar

Cream the butter and sugar together until pale and fluffy. Add the eggs, a little at a time beating well after each addition. Add the flour, spices and baking powder and mix well. Fold in the apples and enough milk to make a soft dropping consistency. Turn the mixture into a greased 20cm (8in) cake tin and bake for about 1½ hrs at gas mark 3, 160°C (325°F) until well risen. Brush the top of the cake with the honey and sprinkle demerara sugar on top.

SPICY CARROT CAKE

This is a healthy, nutritious and yummy cake.

225g, 8oz (2 cups) self-raising wholemeal flour
1 tsp cinnamon
½ tsp nutmeg
½ tsp mixed spice
100g, 4oz (½ cup) butter or margarine
100g, 4oz (⅓ cup) honey
100g, 4oz (1 cup) brown sugar
225g, 8oz carrots, peeled and finely grated

Mix together the flour and spices in a bowl. Melt the butter or margarine, honey and sugar together and stir this into the flour. Next mix in the grated carrot. Put the whole mixture into a well greased 450g (1lb) loaf tin and bake at gas mark 3, 160°C (325°F) for 1½ hours or until a skewer inserted into the centre of the cake comes out clean.

NUTTY CARROT CAKE

4 eggs, separated
100g, 4oz (¹/₃ cup) honey
grated rind and juice of 1 lemon
225g, 8oz carrots, peeled and grated
100g, 4oz (1 cup) hazelnuts, finely chopped
½ tsp cinnamon
a pinch of ground cloves
75g, 3oz (¾ cup) wholemeal flour

Whisk together the egg yolks, honey, lemon rind and juice. Stir in the carrots, nuts, spices and flour. Whisk the egg whites until stiff, then fold into the carrot mixture. Put the mixture into a greased 20cm (8in) square cake tin and bake at gas mark 4, 180°C (350°F) for 25 minutes until golden and firm.

MARMALADE CAKE

100g, 4oz (²/₃ cup) sugar
100g, 4oz (½ cup) margarine
2 eggs, beaten
275g, 10oz (2½ cups) self-raising flour
75g, 3oz (¼ cup) honey
100g, 4oz (¼ cup) marmalade

Cream the fat and the sugar together and add the eggs gradually. Warm the honey and marmalade and stir into the mixture along with the flour. Place in a greased 17.5cm (7in) cake tin and bake in the oven at gas mark 3, 160°C (325°F) for an hour.

ELIZABETHAN PARSNIP CAKE

Parsnips are an unusual ingredient for a cake but, because they are sweet, they work rather well in this cake recipe. This sort of sponge was made in Elizabethan times when honey was the only sweetener and parsnips were added for extra sweetness. The icing is a modern addition.

325g, 12oz (3 cups) self-raising flour
½ tsp bicarbonate of soda
½ tsp nutmeg
2 tsp ground ginger
225g, 8oz parsnips, peeled and grated
150g, 6oz (¾ cup) butter
125g, 5oz (½ cup) honey
1 egg, beaten

Icing

100g, 4oz (¾ cup) icing sugar
a little water

Sift the flour with the bicarbonate of soda, nutmeg and ginger. Melt the butter with the honey and add to the dry ingredients along with the egg. Stir in the parsnips and mix well. Spoon into a greased 17.5cm (7in) cake tin and bake in the oven at gas mark 3, 160°C (325°F) for about 1 hour. Turn out and cool on a wire rack. For the icing, mix the icing sugar with a little water and spread over the top of the cake.

WALNUT CAKE

150g, 6oz (¾ cup) butter
75g, 3oz (¾ cup) brown sugar
3 tbsp honey
3 eggs
150g, 6oz (1½ cups) self-raising flour
75g, 3oz (¾ cup) walnuts

Coffee fudge frosting

50g, 2oz (¼ cup) butter
100g, 4oz (1 cup) brown sugar
3 tbsp coffee essence
2 tbsp single cream
200g, 7oz (1¼ cups) icing sugar

Mix the butter and sugar together in a food processor. Add the flour, eggs and honey. Lastly chop the walnuts and add them to the mixture. Put in a greased 20cm (8in) cake tin and bake in the oven at gas mark 4, 180°C (350°F) for 30 minutes. Turn out onto a wire rack and allow to cool. To make the frosting, melt the butter, sugar, coffee essence and cream in a saucepan and heat gently. Then boil for 3 minutes. Remove from the heat and gradually stir in the icing sugar. Beat with a wooden spoon and continue to beat until thick enough to spread. Ice the cake immediately with this frosting.

SPICY HONEY RING

125g, 5oz (²/₃ cup) margarine
50g, 2oz (½ cup) light brown sugar
3 tbsp clear honey
2 eggs, beaten
150g, 6oz (1½ cups) wholewheat self-raising flour
1 tsp mixed spice
½ tsp ground ginger
75g, 3oz (¾ cup) walnuts, chopped
2 tbsp clear honey for glaze

Beat together the margarine, sugar and honey and then stir in the eggs. Sift the flour and spices and gradually add to the egg mixture along with the walnuts. Spoon the mixture into a greased ring mould and bake in the oven at gas mark 4, 180°C (350°F) for 40 minutes. When cool turn out. Warm the 2 tablespoons of honey and drizzle over the ring.

COFFEE AND HONEY CAKE

150g, 6oz (1½ cups) self-raising flour
2 tsp baking powder
pinch of salt
150g, 6oz (²/₃ cup) margarine
4 tbsp honey
50g, 2oz (¼ cup) caster sugar
3 eggs, beaten
2 tbsp instant coffee

Coffee filling

50g, 2oz (¼ cup) butter
50g, 2oz (¼ cup) icing sugar
1 tsp coffee essence

Sift the flour with the baking powder and salt into a bowl. Add the margarine, honey, caster sugar, eggs and coffee and beat until smooth. Grease two 17.5cm cake tins and place half the cake mixture in each tin. Bake in the oven at gas mark 4, 180°C (375°F) for 25 minutes. Remove from the oven and turn out the cakes onto a wire rack. To make the filling mix together the butter, icing sugar and coffee essence. Sandwich the two cakes together with the filling and dust with icing sugar.

CHOCOLATE CAKE

150g, 6oz (¾ cup) margarine
75g, 3oz (¾ cup) brown sugar
3 tbsp set honey
4 eggs
125g, 5oz (¾ cup) drinking chocolate
125g, 5oz (1¼ cups) self -raising flour

Filling

75g, 3oz (¹/₃ cup) butter
75g, 3oz (½ cup) icing sugar
1 tsp honey

Combine all the cake ingredients in a food processor and process until smooth. Alternatively, cream together the butter, sugar and honey. Then add the eggs, one by one with the flour and drinking chocolate. Mix all well together. Divide between two greased 20cm (8in) cake tins and bake for 30 minutes at gas mark 5, 180°C (375°F). Remove from the cake tins and allow to cool. Beat together the honey, butter and icing sugar and sandwich the two cakes together with the filling. Dust the cake with icing sugar.

HONEY SWISS ROLL

3 eggs
75g, 3oz (¼ cup) set honey
75g, 3oz (¾ cup) self-raising wholemeal flour

Filling

150ml, ¼ pt (²/₃ cup) whipping cream
1 tbsp honey

Beat together the eggs and honey until very thick. Fold in the flour. Pour into a greased and lined Swiss roll tin. Bake in the oven at gas mark 4, 180°C (350°F) for about 10 minutes. Turn the Swiss roll out on to a sheet of greaseproof paper or tea towel sprinkled with caster sugar. Cover with greaseproof paper and roll up with the greaseproof paper in the middle. Leave to cool. Whip the cream with the honey. Unroll and spread with the cream, before rolling up again.

HAZELNUT SWISS ROLL

4 eggs, separated
100g, 4oz (¾ cup) icing sugar
100g, 4oz (1 cup) self-raising flour
100g, 4oz (1 cup) hazelnuts, toasted and crushed
1 tbsp honey
150ml, ¼pt (²/₃ cup) whipped cream

Grease a Swiss roll tin and line with greaseproof paper. Whisk the egg whites and whisk in 50g, 2oz (¹/₃ cup) of the icing sugar. In another bowl, whisk egg yolks with the rest of the icing sugar and then beat in the flour. Fold the egg whites into the egg yolk mixture and spoon onto the tin and spread it out. Bake in the oven at gas mark 5, 190°C (375°F) for 10 minutes. Turn out onto a tea-towel over which you have spread some sugar. Peel off the greaseproof paper. Roll up with the towel inside and cool. Fold the hazelnuts and honey into the cream. Unroll the cake, spread the cream mixture over it and then roll up again. Sprinkle hazelnuts on the top of the Swiss roll if you wish.

HONEY AND LEMON CAKES

These are not particularly elegant cakes but the children will
love them especially if you sandwich them together with
lemon butter filling.

225g, 8oz (2 cups) plain flour
2 tsp baking powder
100g, 4oz (½ cup) margarine
50g, 2oz (⅓ cup) caster sugar
3 tbsp honey
2 eggs, beaten
grated rind and juice of ½ lemon

Butter filling

50g, 2 oz (¼ cup) butter
50g, 2oz (⅓ cup) icing sugar
1 tsp lemon juice

Sift the flour and baking powder into a bowl. Rub in the
margarine. Stir in the sugar. Make a well in the centre of the
flour mixture and gradually beat in the eggs, lemon juice, lemon
rind and honey. The mixture should be stiff but if it is too stiff
and you can hardly mix in all the flour then add a little milk.
When you have mixed everything together well spoon small
amounts of mixture onto greased baking sheets and bake in
the oven at gas mark 5, 190°C (375°F) for about 10 minutes.
Cool on a wire rack and sandwich together with the filling made
by beating butter, icing sugar and lemon juice well together.

BRANDY SNAPS

50g, 2oz (¼ cup) margarine
50g, 2oz (¹/₃ cup) caster sugar
1 tbsp honey
50g, 2oz (½ cup) flour
¼ tsp ground ginger
1 tbsp brandy
whipped cream

Heat the margarine, sugar and honey until melted. Remove from the heat and stir in the flour, ginger and brandy. Place teaspoons of the mixture on a greased baking sheet spacing them well apart. Cook in the oven at gas mark 4, 180°C (350°F) for 10 minutes. Cool slightly and then carefully remove the biscuits with a palette knife and wrap them around an oiled wooden spoon handle. Cool completely and then fill them with whipped cream.

HONEY FLAPJACKS

Children love flapjacks and these have a lovely honey taste.

100g, 4oz (½ cup) margarine
50g, 2oz (½ cup) light brown sugar
3 tbsp set honey
225g, 8oz (3 cups) porridge oats

Melt the margarine, honey and sugar together in a saucepan. Mix in the oats. Press into a greased 27.5 x 17.5cm (11 x 7in) rectangular baking tin and cook in the oven at gas mark 4, 180°C (350°F) for 20 minutes. Cool in the tin and then cut into fingers.

BANANA FLAPJACKS

75g, 3oz (¹/₃ cup) margarine
2 tbsp honey
100g, 4oz (1 cup) brown sugar
1 large, ripe banana, mashed
150g, 6oz (2¹/₃ cups) porridge oats

Put the margarine, honey and sugar in a saucepan and heat gently until the margarine has melted and the sugar dissolved. Then stir in the oats and banana and mix all together. Press into a greased 27.5 x 17.5cm (11 x 7in) rectangular tin and bake in the oven at gas mark 4, 180°C (350°F) for about 30 minutes. Allow to cool in the tin, marking the flapjacks into fingers after they have cooled a little.

HONEY AND APPLE FLAPJACKS

100g, 4oz (½ cup) margarine
50g, 2oz (½ cup) brown sugar
2 tbsp golden syrup
1 tbsp honey
75g, 3oz (1 cup) porridge oats
50g, 2oz (½ cup) wholemeal flour
1 small apple, peeled, cored and grated

Melt the margarine, brown sugar, syrup and honey together and then mix in the oats, flour and grated apple. Press mixture firmly into a greased 27.5 x 17.5cm (11 x 7in) rectangular baking tin and bake in the oven at gas mark 4, 180°C (350°F) for 20 minutes. Allow to cool in the tin before cutting into slices.

BANANA AND CHOCOLATE CRUNCH

Children love this simple biscuit cake.

75g, 3oz (¹/₃ cup) butter
1 tbsp honey
225g, 8oz chocolate digestives, crushed
2 bananas

Melt the butter with the honey. Add the crushed biscuits and bananas chopped small. Put into a tin, spread level and leave in the fridge for at least an hour to set.

PECAN FUDGE BARS

These are very rich and sweet but rather yummy.

150g, 6oz (1½ cups) plain flour
50g, 2oz (½ cup) light brown sugar
75g, 3oz (⅓ cup) butter

Topping

75g, 3oz (⅓ cup) butter
2 tbsp honey
75g, 3oz (¾ cup) dark brown sugar
2 tbsp whipped cream
100g, 4oz (1 cup) pecan nuts

Mix together the flour and sugar and rub in the butter. Press this mixture into a greased 20cm (8in) square baking tin, and bake in the oven at gas mark 4, 180°C (350°F) for 10 minutes. Heat the butter, honey and sugar in a saucepan, bring to the boil and boil for 2 minutes. Remove from the heat and stir in the cream and nuts. Pour over the pastry base and return to the oven for 20 minutes. Take out and allow to cool. The topping will set as it cools.

MUESLI FUDGE SLICES

200g, 7oz tin condensed milk
100g, 4oz (½ cup) butter
125g, 5oz (¾ cup) caster sugar
2 tbsp honey
225g, 8oz (3½ cups) muesli base
150g, 6oz white chocolate

Put the condensed milk, butter, sugar and honey in a saucepan and heat gently until the sugar has dissolved and the butter melted. Then boil gently, stirring until you have a brown frothy mixture. This will take about 5 minutes. Mix in the muesli at once and pour into a well greased 27.5 x 17.5cm (11 x 7in) rectangular tin. Melt the white chocolate and spread over the muesli mixture. Allow to set and then cut into slices.

HONEY MUESLI SLICE

100g, 4oz (¹/₃ cup) clear honey
100g, 4oz (½ cup) butter
75g, 3oz (¾ cup) brown sugar
225g, 8oz (3½ cups) muesli base
50g, 2oz (½ cup) hazelnuts
100g, 4oz plain chocolate

Melt the butter, honey and sugar in a saucepan. Stir in the muesli base and hazelnuts. Mix well. Press the mixture into a greased 20cm (8in) square cake tin and bake in the oven at gas mark 4, 180°C (350°F) for 20 minutes. Take out of the oven. Melt the chocolate over a saucepan of simmering water or in a microwave and use to cover the muesli mixture. Allow to set before cutting into slices.

TOFFEE CHOCOLATE CRUNCH

The children love these and you can always miss out the hazelnuts if you like.

50g, 2oz (¼ cup) butter
2 tbsp honey
100g, 4oz plain or milk chocolate
75g, 3oz bran or wheat flakes
14g, ½oz (1 tbsp) ground or chopped hazelnuts

Melt the butter, honey and chocolate together over a gentle heat. Mix in the bran flakes and hazelnuts. Press into a greased 20cm (8in) square cake tin and leave to set.

CHOCOLATE AND HONEY
BISCUIT CAKE

100g, 4oz (½ cup) margarine
2 tbsp honey
225g, 8oz digestive biscuits, crushed
2 tbsp cocoa powder
50g, 2oz (⅓ cup) caster sugar

Melt the margarine with the honey in a saucepan. Mix together the biscuit crumbs, sugar and cocoa powder. Mix the dry ingredients into the melted margarine and honey. Put into a greased 22.5cm (9in) round or square tin. Smooth the mixture so that it is level and leave to set.

SUNFLOWER AND HONEY CRUNCHES

100g, 4oz (1¾ cups) porridge oats
50g, 2oz (½ cup) sunflower seeds
25g, 1oz (¼ cup) raisins
1 tbsp light soft brown sugar
1 tbsp clear honey
6 tbsp sunflower oil

Mix together the sunflower seeds, oats and raisins. Put the sugar, honey and oil in a saucepan. Heat gently until the sugar has melted. Pour this mixture onto the sunflower seeds, raisins and oats and stir until all the ingredients are well mixed. Put small amounts of the mixture into paper cake cases or into a cake tin for small cakes. Bake in the oven at gas mark 6, (200°C), 400°F for 10 minutes.

SESAME SEED SLICES

100g, 4oz sesame seeds
50g, 2oz (½ cup) plain flour
75g, 3oz (¼ cup) honey
2 tbsp peanut butter
25g, 1oz (¼ cup) demerara sugar

Place all the ingredients in a bowl and mix together. Press into a greased 20cm (8in) square tin and bake in the oven at gas mark 3, 160°C (325°F) for about 40 minutes. Cut into slices and leave in the tin until cool.

PEANUT SHORTBREAD

100g, 4oz (½ cup) butter
125g, 5oz (1¼ cups) wholemeal flour
25g, 1oz (¼ cup) rice flour
50g, 2oz (½ cup) brown sugar
100g, 4oz (1 cup) unsalted peanuts, finely crushed
3 tbsp honey

Mix the flours and sugar together and rub in the butter. Knead until you have a firm dough. Mix together the honey and pea-nuts. Roll out the dough and spread the honey and peanut mixture over it. Roll up so that you have a sausage shape. Then cut into slices about 5mm (¼in) thick. Place on greased baking sheets. Bake in the oven at gas mark 4, 180°C (350°F) for 30 minutes.

PEANUT BUTTER COOKIES

The children will gobble these up. The mixture makes about 18 biscuits. You can always double the quantities if you want more.

1 tbsp honey
65g, 2½oz (¹/₃ cup) margarine
50g, 2oz (½ cup) soft brown sugar
2 tbsp crunchy peanut butter
75g, 3oz (¾ cup) self-raising flour
65g, 2½oz (½ cup) self-raising wholemeal flour

Heat the honey, margarine and sugar together. Stir in the peanut butter and flour. Form the mixture into small balls, place on greased baking sheets and flatten each one slightly with a fork. Cook in the oven at gas mark 4, 180°C (350°F) for 15 minutes. Cool on a wire rack.

PEANUT AND HONEY SQUARES

These are easy and quick to make and children love them.

50g, 2oz (¼ cup) butter
25g, 1oz (¼ cup) brown sugar
4 tbsp honey
4 tbsp crunchy peanut butter
150g, 6oz digestive biscuits, crushed

Put the butter in a saucepan with the sugar and honey and gently heat until everything has melted. Take off the heat and stir in the peanut butter. Add the biscuit crumbs and mix all together. Press the mixture into a greased 20cm (8in) square tin and put in the fridge to set. Cut into squares.

GINGERBREAD MEN

Another treat for the children.

100g, 4oz (1 cup) plain wholemeal flour
½ tsp bicarbonate of soda
½ tsp cinnamon
1 tsp ground ginger
25g, 1oz (2 tbsp) margarine
50g, 2oz (½ cup) brown sugar
1 tbsp clear honey
1 tsp orange juice

Sift the spices and bicarbonate of soda with the flour. Melt the margarine, sugar and honey in a saucepan. Cool and pour onto the flour with the orange juice. Mix to a dough. Roll out to about 5mm (¼in) thick. Use a gingerbread man cutter to cut out the shapes and lay them carefully on a greased baking sheet. Bake in the oven at gas mark 3, 160°C (325°F) for 10 minutes. Decorate as you like.

SHORTBREAD AND HONEY BARS

Base

100g, 4oz (½ cup) butter
150g, 6oz (1½ cups) plain flour
50g, 2oz (⅓ cup) caster sugar

Topping

75g, 3oz (⅓ cup) butter
75g, 3oz (¾ cup) brown sugar
1 tbsp honey
50g, 2oz (½ cup) chopped nuts

Make the shortbread by either combining the butter, flour and sugar in a food processor until they form a dough or rub the margarine into the sugar and flour until the mixture resembles breadcrumbs. Then knead until you have a smooth dough. Press into a greased 27.5 x 17.5cm (11 x 7in) baking tin and bake in the oven at gas mark 4, 180°C (350°F) for about 20 minutes. For the topping melt the butter, sugar and honey in a saucepan and then boil for 3 minutes, stirring constantly. Stir in the nuts and spread this mixture over the shortbread. Leave to set.

HONEYED OATMEAL BISCUITS

25g, 1oz (¼ cup) plain flour
225g, 8oz (1½ cups) oatmeal
50g, 2oz (¼ cup) butter
1 tbsp set honey
pinch of salt

Mix the flour with the oatmeal and salt. Rub in the butter and bind to a firm dough with the honey. Place the pastry between two sheets of greaseproof paper and roll out thinly. Remove the paper and cut into rounds. Place on greased baking trays and cook in the oven at gas mark 4, 180°C (350°F) for 8 - 10 minutes or until crisp and lightly browned.

RICE KRISPIE CRUNCHIES

The children will adore these.

100g, 4oz milk chocolate
2 tbsp honey
50g, 2oz (¼ cup) margarine or butter
75g, 3oz (3½ cups) Rice Krispies

Melt the margarine or butter, honey and chocolate together. Fold in the Rice Krispies and mix well together. Fill paper cases with the mixture and leave to set.

HONEY AND MINCEMEAT
FINGERS

100g, 4oz (1 cup) plain flour
1 tsp baking powder
75g, 3oz (¹/₃ cup) margarine
50g, 2oz (¹/₃ cup) caster sugar
75g, 3oz (1½ cups) porridge oats
2 tbsp set honey
3 tbsp mincemeat

Place all the ingredients except the mincemeat in a bowl and mix to form a dough. Turn onto a floured surface and knead until smooth. Divide in half. Roll out one half and place in a greased 20cm (8in) square tin, then cover it with mincemeat. Roll out the other half and place on top and press down lightly. Bake in the oven at gas mark 4, 180°C (350°F) for about 40 minutes until golden brown. Cool and cut into fingers.

CINNAMON BISCUITS

100g, 4oz (1 cup) wholemeal flour
½ tsp baking powder
1 tsp cinnamon
50g, 2oz (1 cup) porridge oats
75g, 3oz (½ cup) sugar
75g, 3oz (¹/₃ cup) butter
1 tbsp honey
1 tbsp milk

Sift the flour, cinnamon and baking powder together and mix in the oats and sugar. Melt the butter, honey and milk together and beat into the dry ingredients. Shape into small balls and put on a greased baking sheet, flattening them with a fork. Bake in the oven at gas mark 4, 180°C (350°F) for 15 minutes.

HONEY COOKIES

100g, 4oz (½ cup) butter
100g, 4oz (1 cup) soft brown sugar
1 egg
½ tsp vanilla essence
2 tbsp honey
225g, 8oz (2 cups) self-raising wholemeal flour

Cream together the butter and sugar. Gradually add the egg and the vanilla essence. Beat in the honey and add the sifted flour bit by bit until you have a soft dough. Cover and leave in the fridge for an hour. Make balls of the mixture and place on a greased baking sheet, flattening each one a little. Bake in the oven at gas mark 4, 180°C (350°F) for about 10 minutes. Cool on a wire rack.

HONEY NUT COOKIES

25g, 1oz plain chocolate
50g, 2oz (¼ cup) margarine
2 eggs, beaten
4 tbsp honey
100g, 4oz (²/₃ cup) caster sugar
100g, 4oz (1 cup) plain flour
50g, 2oz (½ cup) chopped nuts
½ tsp vanilla essence

Melt the margarine and chocolate together. Add the eggs, honey, sugar, flour, nuts and vanilla essence and mix well. Put small spoonfuls of the mixture on a greased baking sheet and bake in the oven at gas mark 4, 180°C (350°F) for 20 minutes. They will be soft when they come out of the oven but will harden up when cool.

WALNUT COOKIES

150g, 6oz (1½ cups) self-raising flour
75g, 3oz (½ cup) light brown sugar
75g, 3oz (¹/₃ cup) butter
50g, 2oz (½ cup) walnuts, chopped
3 tbsp honey

Sift the flour and add the sugar. Rub in the fat and stir in the walnuts. Add the honey and mix to a firm dough. Form into small balls and place on a greased baking sheet. Bake at gas mark 5, 190°C (375°F) for 15 minutes. Cool on a wire rack.

MUESLI COOKIES

These are not elegant looking biscuits but they are healthy
and the children like them.

125g, 5oz (2 cups) muesli base
25g, 1oz (¼ cup) pecans, finely chopped
50g, 2oz (½ cup) walnuts chopped
1 small apple, grated
50g, 2oz (¹/₃ cup) raisins
25g, 1oz (2 tbsp) margarine
2 tbsp set honey
1 tbsp demerara sugar
1 egg yolk
2 tbsp plain flour

Put the muesli, nuts, grated apple and raisins in a bowl and mix
together. Put the margarine and honey in a small saucepan and
heat until melted. Add to the dry mixture with the sugar and
egg yolk. Add the flour and mix everything so that it binds
together. Shape into round biscuits with your hands. Place on
a greased baking sheet and bake in the oven at gas mark 4,
180°C (350°F) for about 20 minutes.

PRESERVES, SWEETS
AND SAUCES

Rose-Water Honey

Honey Lemon Curd

Honey Marmalade

Honey Fudge

Chocolate and Honey Toffee

Halva

Honey Fudge Sauce

Chocolate Sauce

Orange and Honey Sauce

ROSE-WATER HONEY

This makes a pink honey with a wonderful rose-scented flavour. It is delicious on ice-cream or rice pudding or simply on bread and butter.

600ml, 1pt (2½ cups) rose-water
900g, 2lb (3 cups) clear honey
juice of 1 small lemon
50g, 2oz powdered fruit pectin

Put the honey, rose-water and lemon juice into a saucepan. Stir together and bring to the boil. Simmer for 30 minutes. Sprinkle the pectin over the mixture and boil for 3 minutes. Remove from the heat, and cool a little. Pour into jars and seal well.

HONEY LEMON CURD

4 tbsp honey
3 egg yolks
2 egg whites
rind and juice of 2 lemons
50g, 2oz (¼ cup) butter

Combine all the ingredients in a bowl over a pan of simmering water. Stir the mixture until it thickens. Transfer to a warm clean jar and seal when cold.

HONEY MARMALADE

Makes about 3kg (6.6lb) marmalade

1kg, 2.2lb seville oranges
1litre, 2pts (5 cups) water
675g, 1½lb (2¼ cups) honey
1kg, 2.2lb (6 cups) granulated sugar

Wash the fruit well. Cut in half and extract the juice and flesh. Shred the peel, removing any excess pith. Put the excess pith and pips into a muslin bag. Put the peel, fruit juice, flesh, and water in a large saucepan. Add the muslin bag. Simmer for 2 hours. Squeeze the bag to remove all the juices, add the sugar and honey and stir until the sugar has dissolved. Then boil rapidly until setting point is reached. To find out if the setting point has been reached put a teaspoonful of the marmalade on a plate. If the skin wrinkles on the surface the marmalade is set. Remove from the heat. Stir in a knob of butter to get rid of any foam. Leave to stand for a few minutes and stir to mix in the peel. Pot and seal.

HONEY FUDGE

450g, 1lb (2²/₃ cups) granulated sugar
150ml, ¼pt (²/₃ cup) evaporated milk
65g, 2½oz (¹/₃ cup) butter
3 tbsp honey
a pinch of cream of tartar

Put all the ingredients into a pan over a low heat, stirring all the time until the mixture starts bubbling. Cook for several minutes until a little of the mixture dropped into cold water forms into a ball. Cool the pan quickly by standing in cold water. Beat the mixture with a wooden spoon until it begins to thicken. Pour into a well greased tin and allow to set before cutting into squares.

CHOCOLATE AND HONEY TOFFEE

100g, 4oz (½ cup) butter
225g, 8oz (¾ cup) honey
50g, 2oz (½ cup) soft brown sugar
2 tsp cinnamon
75g, 3oz plain chocolate

Place the honey and sugar in a saucepan and heat gently until the sugar dissolves. Stir in the butter. Boil the mixture until it reaches 132°C (270°F) on a sugar thermometer or drop a little mixture into cold water. Take it out in your fingers and stretch it - it should form hard elastic strands. Take off the heat and mix in the cinnamon. Pour into a greased square tin and allow to cool. When still soft cut into squares. Melt the chocolate and dip the pieces of toffee into the chocolate.

HALVA

This is a traditional Turkish sweetmeat.

100g, 4oz (1 cup) ground almonds
2 tbsp semolina
120ml, 4fl oz (½ cup) milk
2 tbsp honey
1 tbsp butter

Place all the ingredients except the butter in a saucepan and heat gently, stirring all the time. As the liquid begins to thicken, add the butter. You will have a thick paste. Spread evenly into a greased 20cm (8in) square tin, so that the mixture is about 2.5cm (1in) thick. Leave to cool and cut into squares.

HONEY FUDGE SAUCE

This sauce can be served hot or cold. It goes well with ice-cream.

4 tbsp honey
50g, 2oz (¼ cup) butter
75g, 3oz (¾ cup) muscovado sugar
200g, 7oz tin evaporated milk

Melt the ingredients in a saucepan over a gentle heat and when the sugar has dissolved bring to the boil. Boil until the sauce thickens.

CHOCOLATE SAUCE

2 tbsp cocoa powder
4 tbsp honey
50g, 2oz (¼ cup) butter
150ml, ¼pt (²/₃ cup) milk
vanilla essence

Heat all the ingredients gently together until melted. Then bring to the boil and boil for 3 minutes. Serve hot.

ORANGE AND HONEY SAUCE

This can be served with ice-creams, or rice pudding.

1 tsp cornflour
4 tbsp water
3 tbsp orange juice
1 tbsp honey
1 tbsp raisins

Mix the cornflour with a little water. Add the rest of the water and the orange juice. Gently heat this mixture, stirring all the time. Remove from the heat, stir in the honey and raisins and leave to cool.

DRINKS

Honey Toddy

Cider Toddy

Hot Lemon Toddy

Hot Apple and Honey Brew

Eggnog

Honey and Yoghurt All Shook Up

Pineapple and Honey Drink

Tropical Fruit Drink

Spicy Apple Tonic

Kiwi and Honey Cooler

Avocado and Honey Pick-Me-Up

Fruity Punch

Blackberry Vinegar

Walnut Leaf Wine

Dry Still Mead

Sweet Still Mead

HONEY TODDY

Serves 1

300ml, ½pt (1¼ cups) milk
1 tsp honey
1 tbsp whisky

Bring the milk almost to the boil. Stir in the honey and whisky. Drink just before going to bed.

CIDER TODDY

This is a warming drink to have just before going to bed or to warm you up on a cold day.

Serves 1

300ml, ½pt (1¼ cups) dry cider
1 tbsp honey
grated lemon peel
small piece of root ginger

Heat the cider, root ginger and lemon peel in a saucepan until it is just beginning to boil. Remove from the heat, stir in the honey and strain into a mug.

HOT LEMON TODDY

Serves 1

juice of 1 lemon
1 tsp glycerine
1 tbsp honey
water

Put the lemon juice, glycerine and honey in a mug and fill up with boiling water.

HOT APPLE AND HONEY BREW

Serves 4

A great non-alcoholic drink to warm you up in the winter.

1.2l, 2pts (5 cups) apple juice
6 cloves
2 cinnamon sticks
1 tsp nutmeg
3 tbsp honey
4 tbsp lemon juice

Heat all the ingredients together in a large saucepan and bring almost to the boil. Leave to stand for a while. Heat again so that it is the right temperature for drinking and serve at once.

EGGNOG

Serves 1

2 tbsp honey
1 egg
150ml, ¼pt (²/₃ cup) milk
pinch of cinnamon

Beat the honey and egg together and then beat in the milk.
Sprinkle with the cinnamon.

HONEY AND YOGHURT ALL SHOOK UP

Serves 2

1 egg
1 tbsp honey
1 large carton natural yoghurt
juice of 1 orange

Blend all the ingredients together in a blender or food processor. Pour into two glasses and serve at once.

PINEAPPLE AND HONEY DRINK

Serves 1

150ml, ¼pt (²/₃ cup) pineapple juice
1 small carton natural yoghurt
1 tsp clear honey

Whisk the honey, pineapple juice and yoghurt together, and serve in a tall glass.

TROPICAL FRUIT DRINK

Serves 2

300ml, ½pt (1¼ cups) mango juice
flesh of 1 papaya
juice of ½ a lime
2 tbsp honey

Process the mango juice, papaya, lime juice and honey together. Pour into two glasses and serve at once.

SPICY APPLE TONIC

Serves 2

300ml, ½pt (1¼ cups) apple juice
4 cloves
a pinch of cinnamon
1 tbsp honey
300ml, ½ pt (1¼ cups) tonic

Mix the cloves, cinnamon and honey into the apple juice and top up with the tonic.

KIWI AND HONEY COOLER

Serves 1

2 kiwi, puréed
1 tbsp honey
150ml, ¼pt (²/₃ cup) mineral water

Mix the ingredients together and freeze. When ready to serve, take out of the freezer, break up with a fork and put in a glass.

AVOCADO AND HONEY
PICK-ME-UP

This is a highly nutritious vegetable-based juice.

Serves 1

½ an avocado
1 tbsp honey
juice of ½ lemon
150ml, ¼pt (²/₃ cup) soda

Whizz the avocado, honey and lemon together and top up with the soda.

FRUITY PUNCH

Serves 4 - 6

1 bottle of dry white wine
2 tbsp honey
1 peach, sliced
small bunch of cherries, halved and stoned
1 litre of lemonade
mint leaves

Mix all the ingredients together and serve.

BLACKBERRY VINEGAR

This soothes sore throats and colds - take 1 tablespoon in a glass of hot water at bedtime.

600ml, 1pt (2½ cups) white wine vinegar
450g, 1lb (2²/₃ cups) caster sugar
450g, 1lb ripe blackberries
225g, 8oz (¾ cup) honey

Put the blackberries and vinegar in a well sealed jar for one week, shaking a few times each day. Strain into a large saucepan, add the sugar and honey and bring just to the boil. Remove from the heat, stir until the sugar and honey are dissolved and bottle when cool. Cork and store in a cool cupboard.

WALNUT LEAF WINE

I found this interesting recipe in an old Women's Institute edition of Wines, Syrups and Cordials.

1 good handful walnut leaves
3lb demerara sugar
yeast
1 gallon water
1 lb honey

Dissolve the sugar and honey in boiling water. Put the leaves in a bowl and pour on the boiling syrup. Leave for a day. Strain and add the yeast to the liquid. Pour into a sterilised jar and keep in a warm room to ferment. Insert an air lock. Frothing and bubbles will appear which means fermenting has started. When all froth has stopped forming, transfer the jar to a cool room and leave for several days. Syphon off the wine from the yeast deposit and store in a sealed jar in a cellar, or cold room for six months. Then syphon again, bottle, cork and store the bottles for another six months.

DRY STILL MEAD

1.5kg, 3½lb (4¾ cups) mild flavoured honey
mead yeast
5 litres (just over a gallon) water

Heat the mixture of honey and water in a large saucepan until the honey dissolves and bring just to the boil. Cool it and filter through a jelly bag. When cool add the mead yeast. Pour into a clean cask and stand the container in a warm room to ferment. Fermenting starts when you see froth forming. Add more honey water to keep the container full. You will know when fermenting has finished because there will be no more froth or bubbles forming. Clean around the neck of the jar and insert an air lock. Put the cask in a cold room and leave it for two or three weeks. Then syphon off the mead with a sterilised funnel and pour into a sterilised jar or cask. Insert a cork and store for six months. Syphon off the liquid, bottle and cork it. Leave in a cool place, or if possible in a cellar for another six months.

SWEET STILL MEAD

If you would like a sweet still mead you need to store the mead, as prepared above, for at least two years in bottles before sampling. However, there is a danger that the mead may become too sweet.